The Mitchell Beazley
pocket guide to

Aquarium Fishes

Gwynne Vevers

M.B.E., M.A., D.Phil.
Curator of the Aquarium at London Zoo

Mitchell Beazley

Nomenclature

The popular names of fishes vary from one area to another; they are often very misleading and are, of course, useless internationally. The scientific (Latin) name, on the other hand, is governed by strict rules that have been internationally agreed. When a new fish is discovered it is given a double name: the first is the name of the genus (or 'generic' name), the second the name of the species (or 'specific' name), e.g., the Three-spot gourami is *Trichogaster trichopterus*. Each genus contains one or more closely related species. Several related genera are grouped together into a family, families are grouped in suborders, and these are placed in orders.

In some cases a species may be divided into two or more subspecies showing geographical or physical variation. The fishes will then have a third, subspecific, name, e.g., *T. trichopterus sumatranus* (the generic name can be abbreviated the second and subsequent times it is used). Lesser differences are denoted as varieties and are not given a precise scientific name; neither are hybrids, nor fishes that have been selected or domesticated by man, such as the numerous forms of Goldfish and Guppy.

E.g.

Order → **Suborder** → **Family** → **Genus**
Peciformes   Anabantoidei   Osphronemidae   *Trichogaster*

Species
→ *Trichogaster trichopterus* → **Subspecies**
   Three-spot gourami   *Trichogaster trichopterus sumatranus*

Photographs

Cover: **Allan Power/Bruce Coleman**
Heather Angel: 132/133. **Jane Burton/Hans Reinhard/Bruce Coleman:** 13, 14t, 15b, 16b, 17b, 20b, 24b, 25t, 26b, 28t/b, 30t, 32t/b, 34t, 37t, 38b, 39t/b, 41b, 43b, 45t, 46b, 49t, 51t, 52t, 53b, 58b, 63t, 66b, 68t, 69t, 72b, 73t/b, 74b, 75t/b, 76t, 78b, 79b, 90t, 92t, 93t/b, 94t, 95t/b, 96t, 98b, 101t, 102b, 103b, 105b, 106b, 109t/b, 110b, 113b, 114b, 118b, 122b, 123t, 124b, 125t, 126b, 127t, 128b, 130b, 131t, 137t/b, 138t, 141t, 142t, 143t/b, 145t, 146t/b, 148t, 149t, 150b, 151t, 153b, 154b, 158t, 160t/b, 161t, 163t, 164t, 169b, 173t, 174t. **Jacana:** 142b, 154t. **A. van den Nieuwenhuizen:** 17t, 18b, 19t, 21t, 23t, 25b, 27t, 29b, 33b, 35t, 36b, 40b, 42b, 43t, 44t, 45b, 46t, 50b, 54b, 55b, 57b, 60t/b, 62b, 64b, 65t/b, 67t, 71t, 72t, 80m, 82t, 83b, 84t/b, 85t/b, 86t/b, 87b, 88b, 90b, 91t/b, 92b, 97b, 104t, 107b, 112t, 113t, 116t, 117b, 119t/b, 120t, 129b, 131b, 136t/b, 138b, 139t/b, 140t/b, 144t/b, 145b, 147t/b, 148b, 151b, 152t/b, 153t, 155t/b, 156t/b, 157t/b, 158b, 159t/b, 161b, 162t/b, 163b, 164b, 165t/b, 166t/b, 167t/b, 168t/b, 169t, 170t/b, 171t/b, 172t/b, 174b, 175t. **Seaphot:** 67b, 70b, 116b, 141b, 149b. **Zefa:** 150t.

Artwork by Norman Weaver and Eric Tenney
Plant artwork by Jim Channell

Edited and designed by
Mitchell Beazley Publishers Limited
87–89 Shaftesbury Avenue, London W1V 7AD
© Mitchell Beazley Publishers Limited 1980
ISBN 0 85533 209 3
All rights reserved
Typeset by Tradespools Ltd, Frome
Colour reproduction by Lithospeed Ltd
Printed in Great Britain by Jolly and Barber Ltd

Editor Susanne Haines · **Executive Editor** Susannah Read
Art Editor Douglas Wilson · **Production** Julian Deeming

Contents

Introduction

The art of keeping fishes in glass aquarium tanks started in the middle of the nineteenth century when, in May 1853, the Zoological Society of London opened the world's first public aquarium in its Gardens in Regent's Park. This led to the establishment of similar collections and to the foundation of marine biological research stations in all parts of the world. It also stimulated public interest in keeping fishes in private houses and there are now thousands of amateur aquarists in all parts of the world.

Modern methods of heating water and advances in water chemistry have been of great value to aquarists and it is now possible to control the environment of captive fishes far more accurately than that of mammals and birds. The necessary equipment, such as tanks, heaters, thermostats, lighting, aeration pumps and filters, is widely available from aquarium dealers who also sell an extensive range of fishes suitable for the home aquarium. These are mostly flown in from the tropics, particularly from south-east Asia.

The larger tropical fishes, whether freshwater or marine, are more suitable for a public aquarium. The juveniles of such fishes are sometimes kept by home aquarists but these often rapidly outgrow their tank and must then be passed on to a public aquarium.

The breeding of tropical freshwater fishes kept in the aquarium is an achievement that in many cases requires great skill. (See descriptions of individual fishes for the necessary conditions.)

The following pages give general advice on setting up a freshwater aquarium tank; the conditions required for a marine aquarium are discussed on p 134. It is advisable for the beginner to seek practical guidance from an experienced aquarist who can be found by consulting the secretary of one of the numerous aquarist societies. As the beginner gains experience he or she may also want to consult more specialized books on maintenance and breeding.

How to use this book

The freshwater and marine fishes are arranged in evolutionary order, starting with the more primitive species and ending with those that are more advanced or more specialized. The symbols, abbreviations and notes used in the descriptions of the fishes are explained below.

Symbols

♂ male   ♀ female    Recommended for the beginner

Breeding

 Possible or breeds freely    Not recorded or breeds rarely

Tank type (see p 6)

 Community tank    Species tank

Distribution Zoogeographical regions (see map below)

Freshwater fishes

A Australasian   **E** Ethiopian   **N** Nearctic

Nt Neotropical   **O** Oriental   **Pa** Palaearctic

Marine fishes

At Atlantic   **C** Caribbean

IP Indo-West-Pacific Ocean   **M** Mediterranean

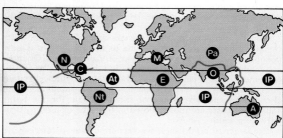

Abbreviations and notes

Length: measurement denotes maximum length of fish reached in the wild

Diet (see p 10)		Water (see p 6)	
cr	small crustaceans	s	soft
in	insects	mh	medium hard
wm	worms	h	hard
vg	vegetable matter	ac	slightly acid
fh	fish	alk	slightly alkaline
mt	meat	nc	not critical
dr	dried foods	pt	peaty
		sal	saline/brackish

Tank: measurement gives recommended length

Anatomy of the fish

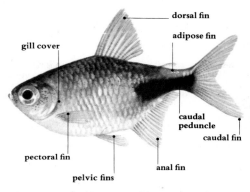

gill cover

dorsal fin

adipose fin

caudal peduncle

caudal fin

pectoral fin

pelvic fins

anal fin

Fishes show a considerable variety of shapes: those that swim fast are torpedo-shaped and their fins are relatively small; bottom-living fishes are flattened; others, such as eels, are long and cylindrical; and there are some bizarre shapes, as in boxfishes, pufferfishes and sea-horses.

The dorsal, caudal and anal *fins* are unpaired; the pectoral and ventral fins are paired—they represent the fore and hind limbs of a mammal. The number and disposition of the spiny or soft rays, which support the fins, are often used to distinguish between similar fishes. In some families, such as the characins, there is a small rayless adipose fin between the dorsal and caudal fins. Most fishes propel themselves by lateral movements of the tail. Some, such as the gobies and wrasses, use the pectoral fins to paddle themselves forwards. Sea-horses move by rapid undulations of the dorsal fin and knifefishes by undulations of the long anal fin.

The *skin* is covered by a layer of mucus which helps to reduce friction during swimming and forms a barrier against infection. Certain fishes, such as naked catfishes, have no scales and in some the body is covered with bony plates. *Coloration* can vary according to mood and general conditions. There are often colour differences between the sexes—these are indicated in the descriptions of individual fishes.

Most fishes have an organ known as the *lateral line*, which can be seen as a thin line along each flank. This consists of a channel, lying below the scales, supplied with numerous nerve endings, and giving off side channels to the surface. It detects pressure waves in the water and enables the fish to locate fixed objects, prey or enemies. Blind fishes orientate themselves by using the lateral line organ.

The *swimbladder* is a gas-filled sac, lying above the gut and below the vertebral column, which serves as a buoyancy organ. The volume of gas can be changed, allowing the fish to adjust its specific gravity to match that of the surrounding water, quite independently of the depth at which it is living. In some species it can also be used as a breathing organ for air swallowed at the surface.

The *gills* are thin-skinned respiratory structures, richly supplied with blood vessels. A current of water passes through the gills where oxygen is absorbed and carbon dioxide released. Some fishes, such as the labyrinth fishes, have accessory air-breathing organs (p 121).

Setting up a freshwater aquarium

Most aquarium fishes are peaceful and can be kept in a 'community tank' (containing two or more species). Some are aggressive or territorial; keep these only with others of their own species in a 'species tank'. (See symbols for individual species.)

An average size for a community tank is about 60 cm long, 30 cm tall and 30 cm wide (volume will vary). When stocking up the tank consider general compatability. By choosing the species carefully you can see that all the water levels are occupied. For example, at the bottom there could be 5–6 Bronze corydoras, in the midwater a small shoal of 5–6 Pearl danios and near the surface 4–5 hatchetfishes.

The tetras and barbs are lively, peaceful and colourful: a group of 4 Glowlight, Neon, Beacon or Lemon tetras and 4 Cherry or Sumatra barbs would make an attractive group with two or three Guppies or Swordtails. A loach would help to clean the tank.

The 'species tank' will provide the best opportunity for experimenting with breeding and observing territorial behaviour.

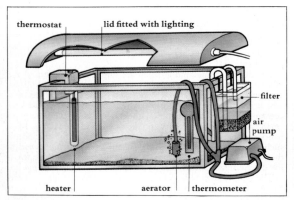

The tank

The most popular tanks are made with glass or clear plastic panes cemented together with silicone glue. Tanks made with an angle iron frame have been used for many years. Do not use a glass 'goldfish bowl'—these are death traps since they have a surface area too small for the volume of water.

A lid will reduce evaporation, prevent dust from settling and—very important—stop fishes from jumping out. Some fishes have a perverse habit of leaping before looking and, without a lid, may be found as desiccated corpses on the floor.

Substrate The bottom of the tank should have a layer of well-washed gravel; sand should be used for burrowing fishes. Some, such as the toothcarps (p 81), need a peat substrate.

Rocks and tree roots These can be arranged to provide shelter. Wash them carefully before use: steep in a weak solution of potassium permanganate and rinse thoroughly. Rocks can be arranged to form small 'caves' in which some species will spawn.

Water

Most tropical aquarium fishes originate from areas where the water is soft and has a low calcium content; however, many fishes can adapt to thrive in hard tap water. But for some species water composition is critical for breeding.

Water hardness refers to the presence of certain salts, primarily calcium and magnesium, expressed in parts per million of calcium carbonate ($CaCO_3$), or on the German scale (°DH) as parts of calcium oxide (CaO) per 100,000 parts.

Water type	$CaCO_3$ (pm)	°DH
soft	0–180	0–10
medium hard	200–320	11–18
hard	340–540	19–30

Aquarium dealers sell kits for determining hardness. Tap water can be softened by adding filtered, unpolluted rain water or de-ionized water (equipment for producing this can be bought). It is usual to replace about a third of the water every month.

Acidity/alkalinity Expressed as the pH (*pondus Hydrogenii*—weight of hydrogen). It can be measured with indicator papers, solutions or with a pH meter. Water at pH 7 is neutral. In the notes on the fishes the term slightly acid means pH 6.0–6.5 and slightly alkaline means pH 7.5–8.0.

Some fishes thrive in brackish water, such as that found in estuaries. This can be simulated by replacing about 10 per cent of the water with a solution made by dissolving two or three teaspoons of sea salt in 10 litres of water.

Heating

Most tropical fishes require a temperature in the range 22–27°C. A thermostat must be used to control the temperature. Wattage should be approximately the same as the volume of the water (e.g., 100 watts for 100 litres). The heater must not touch the tank glass, nor must it be buried in the substrate. A thermometer should be attached to the tank glass by a rubber suction pad.

N.B. A tank for cold-water fishes must not be heated.

Aeration

Natural waters usually contain sufficient oxygen for fishes—in an aquarium there may at times be a deficiency. Introducing a stream of compressed air bubbles, produced by one of the many commercially available air pumps will remedy this. Although only a very small percentage of the oxygen in the bubbles becomes dissolved in the water, aeration is of great value as it continually pushes new water to the surface where oxygen is absorbed and carbon dioxide released.

Filtration

This is not necessary in a well-maintained tank. It does not purify the water; it merely removes visible waste matter. Nylon wool, peat and charcoal are common filter media, contained in a box inside or outside the tank. An external filter is preferable. There is also a biological system which filters water through the substrate.

Peat filtration is an excellent method. Aquarium dealers supply an acid peat, which softens the water and lowers the pH— important for certain 'difficult' fishes. Renew every 6–8 weeks.

Lighting

Illuminate the tank for 12–16 hours each day, using fluorescent lights mounted in fittings with a reflector above a sheet glass lid, or under the hood of a moulded lid. Do not switch on the lights suddenly if the room is dark as this scares the fishes. Artificial lighting encourages plant growth but daylight encourages algal growth and cannot, of course, be controlled. The tank can, however, be left in daylight for up to two weeks if the aquarist is on holiday.

Before introducing your fishes into the aquarium allow the water to settle for about one week and check that all the equipment is in good working order. Use a net to transfer the fishes—they should not be handled.

Plants

An aquarium can be made more attractive by having groups of plants (obtainable from aquarium dealers). Some are true aquatic plants, others are marsh plants which can tolerate total submersion. Floating plants provide shelter for shy fishes and for the eggs and fry. Aquarium plants are usually planted in the substrate in groups, allowing plenty of space for the fishes to swim in.

There is a widespread belief that plants are useful as oxygenators in the aquarium. This is not strictly true. In a lit aquarium they certainly give off oxygen and take up some of the carbon dioxide produced by the fishes. However, at night this process is reversed. Plants are, therefore, primarily for decoration.

Most of the plants illustrated can be propagated by cuttings or by replanting runners anchored by small rocks or glass rods until they have rooted. A gravel or sand substrate is usually suitable although an addition of a little loam is sometimes necessary—this will not harm the fishes.

Cabomba aquatica
America: with finely divided leaves. Needs good light. Propagate by cuttings

Cryptocoryne affinis
Malaya: with fairly broad leaves, up to 50 cm long. Slow growing

Ceratopteris thalictroides
A floating fern, with broad-leaved and fine-leaved forms. Daughter plantlets are produced at the edges of the leaves. Can be planted in the substrate

Echinodorus magdalenensis
The Dwarf Amazon sword plant. Has pale green tough leaves. Produces long runners with plantlets. Fast growing

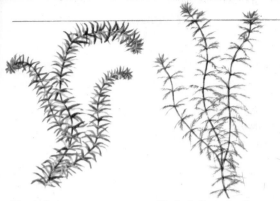

Egeria densa
South America: with small leaves arranged in whorls. In good light and fairly hard water it grows rapidly

Myriophyllum aquaticum
America: one of the milfoils, with pale green, much divided leaves. A useful spawning site for some fishes

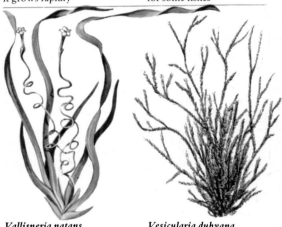

Vallisneria natans
Asia: with long (up to 1 m), tough, strap-like leaves. One of several forms grown in the aquarium

Vesicularia dubyana
Java moss from south-east Asia. Grows attached to rocks or tree roots. Needs good light

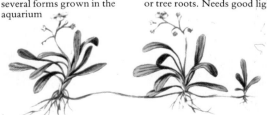

Sagittaria subulata
America: long, strap-like submerse leaves and broader floating leaves. Plant in sand with a little loam

9

Feeding

Overfeeding is a hazard: excess food decomposes rapidly and pollutes the water. Only give the fishes as much food as they will consume in 10–15 minutes once a day (or less frequently, depending on the species). This applies particularly to dried foods. In an established tank most species can be left for up to two weeks without being fed.

Food for adults and juveniles

Live food Includes tiny crustaceans, such as water-fleas (*Daphnia*) and *Cyclops*, mosquito and gnat larvae, which can all be found in ponds during summer. Whiteworms (*Enchytraeus*) are available throughout the year but they are a rich, fatty food and should be fed in moderation. *Tubifex* worms can be collected from river-beds, particularly in muddy places, or they may be bought from a dealer. Wash them thoroughly, leaving them in a bowl under running water for at least 48 hours. Fruitflies (*Drosophila*) can be found on and around rotting fruit and are quite easy to breed. Place a few of these flies in a milk bottle or jar with a small amount of mashed banana and close the top with cotton wool. The flies lay eggs which hatch into larvae that feed on the banana. These develop into pupae from which the new fruitflies emerge.

Larger live food includes woodlice, bluebottles, water insects and their larvae (such as dragonfly nymphs), caterpillars (not hairy ones), earthworms, tadpoles and small fishes (some aquarists use unwanted young Guppies).

Animal foods Grated cooked beef heart and chopped fish flesh are used.

Dried foods These include oatflakes, hard-boiled egg yolk and dried yeast, as well as numerous commercial brands in flake or powder form. Increasing use is made of freeze-dried food, broken up into sizes suitable for the fishes concerned.

Vegetable matter Certain fishes require a supplement of vegetable matter and some feed almost exclusively on plant foods. The most widely used are carefully washed lettuce leaves, boiled spinach and soaked oatflakes. In addition, the natural growth of algae in the tank is often appreciated.

Food for fry

Infusorians The very tiny fry of certain fishes are fed on a type of food known as infusorians. These include many microscopic animals such as rotifers which are abundant in ponds, and the slipper animalcule *Paramecium* which is a single-celled animal, or protozoan. *Paramecium* can be cultured in a glass vessel (never in a fish tank). Soak a small quantity of hay or chopped turnip for two or three days in rain or pond water. The culture will become pink. It does not survive long in warm water and should be transferred in small amounts to the fish tank using a pipette.

Brine shrimp nauplii The newly hatched nauplii or larvae of the brine shrimp (*Artemia salina*) are invaluable for larger fish fry. Brine shimp eggs are widely available in aquarium shops. Place about half a teaspoon of eggs in one litre of water with a tablespoon of ordinary salt. Aerate briskly. If kept at approximately 24°C they should hatch in about 30 hours. Transfer the nauplii to separate small vessels and feed on just enough yeast to make the water slightly cloudy. The water will slowly become clearer as the nauplii filter out the microscopic yeast cells.

The fry will gradually accept larger food.

Breeding

This is an area which presents the amateur aquarist with his or her greatest challenge. In the wild most tropical fishes breed at any time of the year. This also applies in the aquarium and will often be successful provided suitable food for the newly hatched fry is available. Some general hints on breeding are given here for the majority of fishes that shed their eggs at random in the water.

Some species spawn more readily when the weather is fine, some when the sun shines on the tank in the early morning.

The breeding pair must be healthy, with typical body shape, pattern and coloration. They must be fed a varied diet of live food. It is best to choose a pair that have shown courtship behaviour in a community tank. The female should have a rounded belly, indicating her readiness to spawn.

The breeding tank should be all glass, without a metal frame. It must be carefully cleaned and have a substrate of well-washed gravel. For those species which spawn among vegetation there should be a few plants of *Myriophyllum* (milfoil). Some aquarists use a mop of nylon wool as a spawning site.

Although most tropical fishes will live and grow quite happily in tap water many of them will only breed in soft, slightly acid water. This can be simulated by diluting tap water with filtered rain water or preferably with distilled or de-ionized water (see p 6). The tank should be allowed to settle for a few days before the breeding pair is introduced. Mating behaviour varies but may involve rapid swimming movements or chasing and circling by the male.

When the eggs are laid at random they may be difficult to see as they are small and transparent. They can be detected by shining a light through the back pane of the tank when they will show up as minute glistening spheres. Eggs laid on leaves or rocks are usually quite easily seen. Dead or infertile eggs are opaque and should be removed at once with a pipette.

Several aquarium fishes are notorious for the habit of eating their own eggs. In such cases it is best to remove the parents immediately after spawning. The breeding tank should then be kept in subdued light and the eggs will usually hatch in a few days; in some species the eggs hatch in about 24 hours. The newly hatched fry hang from plants or the tank glass or lie on the bottom for a short period during which they live on the contents of the yolk sac. They then assume the normal horizontal position and become free-swimming. At this point they can be fed on small quantities of very fine food such as infusorians or brine shrimp nauplii. When they have started to feed satisfactorily the fry can be transferred to another tank for rearing, using a wide-mouthed pipette. Replace about 10 per cent of the water in this tank with water of the same composition as that in the community tank and repeat several times to acclimatize the young fish to the conditions in a community tank.

The breeding pair can be put together again for a further spawning when the female shows a well-rounded belly.

There are more specialized methods of breeding: several species guard and tend their eggs and fry; some lay eggs in neat groups on leaves or rocks; some in floating nests of air bubbles coated with saliva (e.g., labyrinth fishes). In others one of the parents, usually the female, incubates the eggs in her mouth (e.g., some cichlids). In the live-bearing fishes, which are mostly members of the family Poeciliidae, the female produces batches of live young (e.g., Guppy, Platy and Swordtail). Further information is given in the descriptions of the individual fishes and the family introductions.

11

Disease

Disease often occurs when the fish has lost resistance, usually due to factors in the environment. These include overcrowding, unsuitable food, low water temperature, sudden fluctuations in temperature, lack of oxygen and the presence of toxic substances (such as insecticides and tobacco smoke). The microscopic organisms in the water soon gain the upper hand and multiply rapidly.

A wounded fish may be attacked by fungus which appears as a thin mould covering the skin. Remove the fish immediately to a separate tank and bathe it in a solution of aureomycin (13 mg per 1.2 litres). Alternatively, infected fishes can be removed and dabbed once a day with 5 per cent methylene blue.

White spot

The commonest aquarium disease is white spot, or itch, caused by the protozoan *Ichthyophthirius multifiliis*. It frequently appears when there has been a drop in the temperature of the water. White spots, 0.5–1 mm across, develop on the skin and fins. The fishes may start to rub against the rocks, and the spots or cysts drop off and fall to the bottom. There they form large numbers of free-swimming, microscopic parasites which infect other fishes. This is the stage at which they can be killed by one of many preparations sold by aquarium dealers but action must be taken very promptly.

Velvet disease

The second most common disease is velvet, caused by the microscopic organism *Oodinium limneticum*. It appears on the skin as powdery golden spots. This parasite contains chlorophyll and can live for quite a time in a lit tank, even when there are no fishes. It commonly attacks barbs, danios and labyrinth fishes. Isolate infected fishes in a separate tank, without plants, and treat them for about 10 days with a 5 per cent solution of methylene blue. The original infected tank must be thoroughly cleaned, the plants washed in potassium permanganate and the water, of course, discarded.

Fish tuberculosis

This is not uncommon, particularly in the domesticated varieties of the Guppy and Siamese fighting fish. The fish swims slowly, often off balance and red areas can be detected on the gills. An infected fish should be removed but it is not yet really possible to effect a cure. Very rarely this disease causes a skin rash on humans, which may last a long time but is not dangerous.

Dropsy

The condition known as dropsy is due to the accumulation of fluids in the body. This causes the scales to stick out from the body surface. It is probably caused by a virus infection and can sometimes be cured by treatment with chloramphenicol (250 mg to 4.5 litres of water).

The chemicals mentioned here are available from a pharmacist who will measure them out for you. Aureomycin and chloramphenicol require a prescription.

Freshwater fishes

Brightly coloured fishes living in a well-kept aquarium are a source of endless fascination. Remember that a fish's appearance often reflects the conditions in which it is kept so make sure that you follow the recommended requirements. The same species can show considerable colour variation—age, diet, tank conditions and even mood all contribute—so do not be alarmed if the illustrations do not match your fishes exactly.

Family Polypteridae

Restricted to tropical Africa. The dorsal fin is broken up into several finlets; the paddle-like pectoral fins are used in swimming and to support the body when at rest. The swimbladder is used as an accessory breathing organ for air swallowed at the surface.

Reedfish

Erpetoichthys calabaricus

This peaceful, nocturnal species moves rather like a snake over the bottom of the tank, rising to the surface at intervals to breathe air. It is hardy, but rather shy. Male has 12–14, female has 9–12 anal fin rays. Niger delta, Cameroon. *Length:* to 90 cm; *Diet:* cr, in, wm; *Water:* nc, 22–27°C; *Tank:* 80 cm

Family Osteoglossidae

Found in South America, Africa, Malay Peninsula and Australia. This distribution is evidence of a former land-bridge between the continents. Probably able to breathe air using the swimbladder.

Arawana

Osteoglossum bicirrhosum

No external sex differences

Large bony scales

Only young specimens are suitable for the home aquarium as they grow rapidly; larger specimens make good exhibits in public aquaria. The tank must have a well-fitting lid as the fishes tend to leap. Keep only with larger fishes. The Guianas, Amazon basin. *Length:* to 100 cm; *Diet:* cr, in, fh, dr; *Water:* s, 24–29°C; *Tank:* 70 cm

Family Pantodontidae

Only one species from West Africa, living in slow-flowing rivers and weedy lakes. Thought to be related to the Osteoglossidae.

Butterflyfish

Pantodon buchholzi

Does not flap pectoral fins when gliding

Mainly active at night

♂ has a concave anal fin

Takes insects from the surface in its huge upward-directed mouth

A surface-living fish, it leaps and glides for short distances through the air, with the wing-like pectoral fins spread out. The young are difficult to rear as they require very tiny live food such as infusorians. Niger, Cameroon, Zaïre. *Length:* to 10 cm; *Diet:* cr, in, fh; *Water:* s, ac, pt, 23–29°C; *Tank:* 60 cm

Family Notopteridae

Knifefishes: five species found in Africa and south-east Asia, living in quiet backwaters. They become active at night, hunting small prey on the river-bed. Undulations of the long anal fin enable the fishes to move equally well backwards and forwards.

African knifefish

Xenomystus nigri

At rest these fishes assume an oblique position with head down. This nocturnal species should be kept as a small shoal. Rises to the surface to swallow air. Liberia to Nile basin. *Length:* to 30 cm; *Diet:* cr, in, wm, mt; *Water:* s, ac, pt, 24–28°C; *Tank:* 80 cm

Family Mormyridae

Found only in Africa, some species live on the river-bed, others (without the trunk-like snout) in midwater. The brain is very large (proportionately as large as man's). These fishes were depicted in Egyptian tombs *c.* 2500 BC.

Elephant nose

Gnathonemus petersi

Mainly active in twilight

No external sex differences

Elongated snout is used for digging

Weak electric organs situated in the rear part of the body emit electric pulses that are used in navigation and probably help to define territories. The tank should have rocks to provide hiding places and lighting should be subdued. Niger, Cameroon, Zaïre. *Length:* to 23 cm; *Diet:* cr, in, dr; *Water:* nc, 24–28°C; *Tank:* 60 cm

Family Gymnarchidae

One species only, found in Africa. As in the Mormyridae there are weak lateral electric organs that are used in navigation more effectively than the small eyes. The electric pulses define objects and are also used to detect food.

Gymnarchus niloticus

Reversible undulations of the dorsal fin enable this fish to move backwards and forwards equally well. Field observations in The Gambia showed that this fish makes a floating nest of plant fragments in which the female lays about 1,000 eggs. Senegal to Niger, Chad basin, upper Nile. *Length:* to 90 cm; *Diet:* cr, in, wm; *Water:* nc, 23–26°C; *Tank:* 90 cm

Family Characidae

The characins, a family of about 1,350 species (found mostly in tropical America, a few in central Africa), contain many attractive fishes which are very popular with the aquarist. None has barbels but most have a small adipose fin. The habits of this family are variable: most are carnivorous, some omnivorous or herbivorous. Most have been bred successfully for many years; they require few special conditions and will spawn at random, the eggs being fertilized in the water. Soft, slightly acid water is preferable. A community tank is suitable for most species except for the aggressive piranhas and related species (which are sometimes placed in a separate family, the Serrasalmidae).

Piranha

Pygocentrus piraya

This and the two following species have extremely sharp, powerful teeth. They hunt in shoals and are able to reduce prey, even a horse, to a skeleton in minutes. They are thought to be attracted to animals which are bleeding. More suitable for a public aquarium. R. Orinoco, Guyana, R. Amazon, R. Paraguay, R. de la Plata. *Length:* to 35 cm; *Diet:* in, wm, fh, mt; *Water:* s, ac, pt, 24–27°C; *Tank:* 80 cm

Red piranha

Serrasalmus nattereri

Coloration is very variable but the underparts are bright red. Guyana, basins of Amazon, Orinoco, and Paraná. *Length:* to 30 cm; *Diet:* in, wm, fh, mt; *Water:* s, ac, pt, 24–26°C; *Tank:* 80 cm

White piranha

Serrasalmus rhombeus

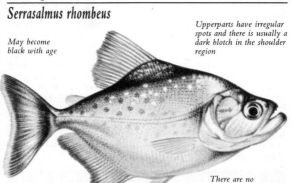

May become black with age

Upperparts have irregular spots and there is usually a dark blotch in the shoulder region

There are no external sex differences

This is an unsociable fish, which can be particularly aggressive towards weaker members of its own species. It is suitable for the home aquarium only when young. Guyana, Amazon basin. *Length:* to 35 cm; *Diet:* in, wm, fh, mt; *Water:* s, ac, pt, 24–26°C; *Tank:* 80 cm

Bloodfin

Aphyocharax rubripinnis

♂ slimmer and more colourful during breeding period

This species is easy to breed. Spawning usually takes place soon after dawn. Remove the parent fishes as they will eat the eggs which sink to the bottom and hatch in 24–26 hours. The fry hang at the water surface for a few days and should be fed on brine shrimp nauplii. Argentina. *Length:* to 5.5 cm; *Diet:* cr, in, wm, dr; *Water:* s–mh, 18–28°C; *Tank:* 30 cm

Diamond tetra

Moenkhausia pittieri

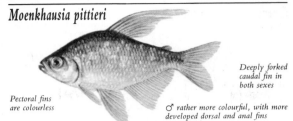

Deeply forked caudal fin in both sexes

Pectoral fins are colourless

♂ *rather more colourful, with more developed dorsal and anal fins*

A hardy, very productive species, best kept as a small shoal. It has been known to breed in quite a small tank (20 litres). The young can be fed on brine shrimp nauplii as soon as they are free-swimming. L. Valencia (Venezuela). *Length:* to 6 cm; *Diet:* cr, in, wm, dr; *Water:* s–mh, 22–26°C; *Tank:* 40 cm

Red-eye tetra

Moenkhausia sanctaefilomenae

Lives mainly in the middle water

♂ *is smaller and more slender*

Upper half of eye is brilliant blood-red

Belly profile is more convex in ♀

The body has an iridescent silvery sheen. The dorsal fin and the front rays of the anal fin have whitish tips and there is a dark transverse band at the base of the tail. This is a lively shoaling fish which mixes well with other peaceable tetras. Paraguay, R. Paranaíba. *Length:* to 7 cm; *Diet:* cr, in, wm, vg, dr; *Water:* s–mh, 20–26°C; *Tank:* 50 cm

Black tetra

Gymnocorymbus ternetzi

♀

The dark pigment, mostly towards the rear, becomes greyer as the fish ages

Lives in the upper and middle water

♂ is smaller than ♀, its caudal fin marked with white spots

When viewed against the light the body cavity is pointed posteriorly in the male and rounded in the female. The characteristic curved anal fin is almost as long as the rear half of the body. This area becomes greyer with age. These fishes are not difficult to breed and should be kept in a small shoal. R. Negro, R. Paraguay. *Length:* to 5.5 cm; *Diet:* cr, in, wm, dr; *Water:* s–mh, 23–25°C; *Tank:* 40 cm

Boehlke's penguin fish

Thayeria boehlkei

Oblique swimming position is characteristic. The longitudinal black stripe extends from behind the gill cover to the base of the tail where it curves downwards and ends at the tip of the lower caudal fin lobe. Best kept in a small shoal. Amazon basin. *Length:* to 8 cm; *Diet:* cr, in, wm, dr; *Water:* s–mh, 23–27°C; *Tank:* 50 cm

Penguin fish

Thayeria obliquua

Very similar to *T. boehlkei* but the longitudinal stripe starts behind the dorsal fin. The male is slimmer than the female. This prolific fish, capable of producing broods of 1,000 or more, spawns among fine-leaved plants and the brown eggs hatch in 12–20 hours. Amazon basin. *Length:* to 8 cm; *Diet:* cr, in, wm, dr; *Water:* s, ac, 23–27°C; *Tank:* 50 cm

X-ray fish

Pristella riddlei

Best kept as a shoal

♂

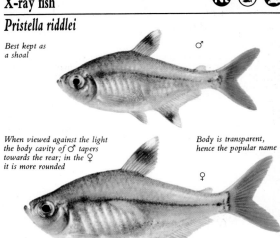

When viewed against the light the body cavity of ♂ tapers towards the rear; in the ♀ it is more rounded

Body is transparent, hence the popular name

♀

Provided a compatible pair can be found, this species is quite easy to breed. Spawning should take place preferably in subdued light. The female may produce 300–400 eggs. A few days after hatching the fry can be fed on brine shrimp nauplii. Venezuela, Guyana, lower Amazon. *Length:* to 4.5 cm; *Diet:* cr, in, wm, dr; *Water:* s–mh, 20–26°C; *Tank:* 40 cm

Buenos Aires tetra

Hemigrammus caudovittatus

♂ is slimmer and more colourful

Fins of ♀ are almost colourless

♂

An old favourite, introduced into the aquarium world around 1922. For breeding the optimum temperature is 23–25°C and spawning is often encouraged when the aquarium receives the morning sun. A greedy fish. R. de la Plata. *Length:* to 12 cm; *Diet:* cr, in, wm, vg, dr; *Water:* s, ac, pt, 18–28°C; *Tank:* 40 cm

Glowlight tetra

Hemigrammus erythrozonus

♀ is larger and stouter than ♂

Inhabits the lower half of the tank

Striking iridescent red 'glowlight' at tail-base

Not easy to spawn although it can sometimes be done in the dark in soft, slightly acid water, a proportion of which should be changed at intervals as the young are growing. North-eastern South America. *Length:* to 4.5 cm; *Diet:* cr, wm, vg, dr; *Water:* s, ac, pt, 24–28°C; *Tank:* 40 cm

Green neon

Hemigrammus hyanuary

♂ is smaller and more slender

Iris may be grass-green

Characteristic iridescent stripe along the flanks

Fins are transparent (except front of anal fin)

A recent introduction to the aquarium. Prefers to spawn (usually at twilight) among fine-leaved plants in a carefully cleaned tank without substrate. L. Hyanuary (Brazil). *Length:* to 4 cm; *Diet:* cr, wm, vg, dr; *Water:* s, ac, pt, 24–26°C; *Tank:* 30 cm

Beacon fish

Hemigrammus ocellifer

When viewed against the light the whole of the swimbladder is visible in the male, whereas only part may be seen in the female. A large tank (over 50 litres) is necessary as this is a very prolific fish. Orinoco and Amazon basins. *Length:* to 4.5 cm; *Diet:* cr, in, wm, vg, dr; *Water:* s, ac, pt, 22–27°C; *Tank:* 30 cm

Pretty tetra

Hemigrammus pulcher

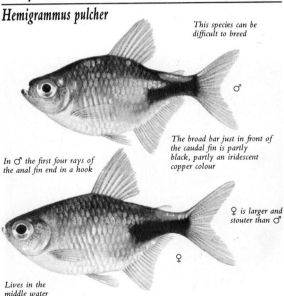

This species can be difficult to breed

♂

The broad bar just in front of the caudal fin is partly black, partly an iridescent copper colour

In ♂ the first four rays of the anal fin end in a hook

♀ is larger and stouter than ♂

♀

Lives in the middle water

A peaceful fish which can be prolific. It is not always easy to find a reliable breeding pair and the male should be replaced if spawning fails. Lower Amazon. *Length:* to 4.5 cm; *Diet:* cr, wm, vg, dr; *Water:* s, ac, pt, 23–26°C; *Tank:* 30 cm

...tra

rhodostomus

♀ *is larger and stouter than* ♂

... the fish is in good condition

Also known as the Rummy-nosed tetra. A difficult fish to breed, the recommended softness of the water being about 3°DH. Few eggs are laid and these hatch in 30–36 hours. Best kept as a shoal. A substrate of boiled peat should be provided. Lower Amazon. *Length:* to 4 cm; *Diet:* cr, wm, vg, dr; *Water:* s, ac, pt, 23–26°C; *Tank:* 30 cm

False rummy-nose

Petitella georgiae

♂ *is slimmer and smaller than* ♀

Lives in the middle and lower waters and best kept as a shoal

Very similar to *H. rhodostomus*, although the central black tail marking does not extend so far forward and there are differences in the arrangement of the teeth. The similarity has caused much confusion in the aquarium world. Iquitos area (upper Amazon, Peru). *Length:* to 5 cm; *Diet:* cr, wm, vg, dr; *Water:* 23–25°C; *Tank:* 30 cm

24

Blood characin

Hyphessobrycon callistus

The male is smaller and more brightly coloured than the female. There are several different Blood characins, varying in coloration and markings, which are regarded by some authorities as subspecies of *H. callistus*. They are attractive fishes which breed well. Amazon, upper Paraguay. *Length:* to 4.5 cm; *Diet:* cr, in, wm, vg, dr; *Water:* s, 23–25°C; *Tank:* 30 cm

Griem's tetra

Hyphessobrycon griemi

♂ is shorter and more slender than ♀

Similar to H. flammeus *(p 26) but a much later introduction to the aquarium (c. 1956), and rather less colourful, although the body becomes redder when the fish is excited*

This species is best kept as a small shoal and is not difficult to breed. The eggs hatch in 24–40 hours and the fry hang from the tank vegetation for about 5 days. They can then be fed on tiny live food, such as infusorians. Goiáz (Brazil). *Length:* to 3 cm; *Diet:* cr, wm, vg, dr; *Water:* s–mh, 22–26°C; *Tank:* 40 cm

Flame tetra

Hyphessobrycon flammeus

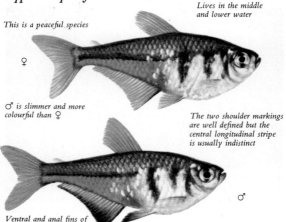

This is a peaceful species

Lives in the middle and lower water

♀

♂ is slimmer and more colourful than ♀

The two shoulder markings are well defined but the central longitudinal stripe is usually indistinct

♂

Ventral and anal fins of ♂ are edged with black

This species was introduced to the aquarium *c.*1920. Best kept in a small shoal, it is an undemanding fish which breeds easily, even in medium–hard tap water. The female may produce up to 300 eggs, which hatch in two to three days. The fry hang from plants for 3 to 4 days. Rio de Janeiro area (Brazil). *Length:* to 4.5 cm; *Diet:* cr, wm, vg, dr; *Water:* s–mh, 21–25°C; *Tank:* 40 cm

Black neon

Hyphessobrycon herbertaxelrodi

The prominent longitudinal band consists of an upper iridescent stripe and a lower deep black stripe. This species has not often been bred in captivity and is said not to be prolific, although broods of up to 180 have been reported. R. Taquári (Brazil). *Length:* to 4.5 cm; *Diet:* cr, wm, vg, dr; *Water:* s, ac, 24–27°C; *Tank:* 30 cm

Flag tetra

Hyphessobrycon heterorhabdus

The male is smaller and has a more tapered body cavity at the rear end than the female. A somewhat delicate fish that is not always easy to keep in large numbers and not usually prolific. Lower Amazon, R. Tocantins. *Length:* to 5 cm; *Diet:* cr, wm, vg, dr; *Water:* s, ac, 23–26°C; *Tank:* 30 cm

Ornate tetra

Hyphessobrycon ornatus

This high-backed characin swims mostly in the lower waters

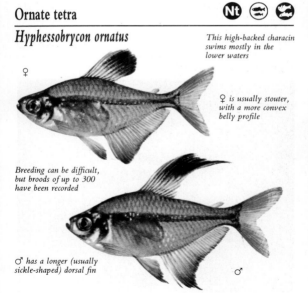

♀ *is usually stouter, with a more convex belly profile*

Breeding can be difficult, but broods of up to 300 have been recorded

♂ *has a longer (usually sickle-shaped) dorsal fin*

This fish has the reputation of being difficult to breed and it is possible that some males are sterile. The breeding tank should have a volume of at least 30 litres. A peaceful shoaling fish which is easy to keep. Guyana. *Length:* to 6 cm; *Diet:* cr, in, vg, dr; *Water:* s, 23–26°C; *Tank:* 30 cm

Lemon tetra

Hyphessobrycon pulchripinnis

This species spawns well when the female is given a rich, varied diet. The male is more slender and the anal fin has a broad black edge which is absent in the female. South America (exact location unknown). *Length:* to 5 cm; *Diet:* cr, wm, vg, dr; *Water:* s, 23–25°C; *Tank:* 30 cm

Bleeding heart tetra

Hyphessobrycon rubrostigma

The male is smaller, slimmer and more colourful than the female. Provide plenty of vegetation as this helps to prevent the fishes from becoming shy. Best kept as a small shoal and fed on a varied diet of live food. Not an easy fish to breed. Colombia. *Length:* to 6 cm; *Diet:* cr, wm, vg, dr; *Water:* s, 23–25°C; *Tank:* 40 cm

Black-line tetra

Hyphessobrycon scholzei

♂ is more slender and
has darker markings

*This is a peaceful
shoaling fish*

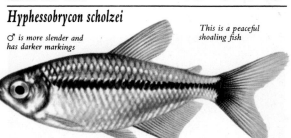

This is one of the easiest tetras to breed and is therefore suitable for the beginner. The breeding tank should be allowed to settle for one or two weeks before the fishes are introduced in the evening. They usually spawn the following morning. The male has a more deeply forked tail. Pará (Brazil). *Length:* to 5 cm; *Diet:* cr, wm, vg, dr; *Water:* s–mh, 23–25°C; *Tank:* 50 cm

Two-spot astyanax

Astyanax bimaculatus

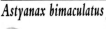

*Keep in a
small shoal*

Numerous races and colour varieties have developed within the wide distribution range of this species. Usually swims in the lower and middle water. North-eastern South America. *Length:* to 15 cm; *Diet:* cr, in, wm, dr; *Water:* nc, 23–26°C; *Tank:* 60 cm

Blind cave characin

Astyanax mexicanus

Formerly known as *Anoptichthys jordani*, this subterranean cave-dwelling fish is now regarded as a blind form of *Astyanax mexicanus*, which occurs from Texas to Panama. The lateral line is used for orientation. It will mate with normally sighted forms. San Luis Potosí (Mexico). *Length:* to 6 cm; *Diet:* cr, in, wm, dr; *Water:* mh, alk, 18–25°C; *Tank:* 60 cm

Silver tetra

Ctenobrycon spilurus

Tends to eat the leaves of soft plants and nibbles the fins of other fishes (especially Angelfishes)

Conspicuous blue-black marking on shoulder

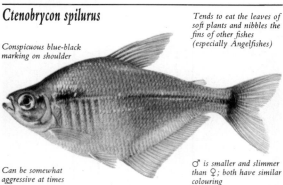

Can be somewhat aggressive at times

♂ is smaller and slimmer than ♀; both have similar colouring

This hardy, prolific species is best kept as a shoal in a well-planted tank. After a vigorous courtship among the plants, the female spawns readily, sometimes producing up to 1,000 eggs in a single spawning. At a temperature of 26°C the eggs will hatch in 24 hours. Care should be taken to prevent the parent fishes from eating them. Coastal areas of Venezuela, Guyana and Surinam. *Length:* to 9 cm; *Diet:* cr, in, wm, vg, dr; *Water:* nc, 20–27°C; *Tank:* 50 cm

Emperor tetra

Nematobrycon palmeri

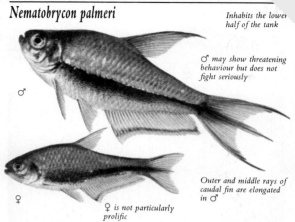

Inhabits the lower half of the tank

♂ *may show threatening behaviour but does not fight seriously*

♂

Outer and middle rays of caudal fin are elongated in ♂

♀

♀ *is not particularly prolific*

Tends to be territorial, rather than living in a shoal. Breeding is a bit unreliable and depends on finding a compatible pair. The few eggs produced by the female are laid among the tank vegetation. These hatch in 24–28 hours and after about 5 days the fry will feed on tiny live food. R. San Juan (Colombia). *Length:* to 6 cm; *Diet:* cr, in, wm, mt, dr; *Water:* s, ac, 24–26°C; *Tank:* 30 cm

Disc tetra

Ephippicharax orbicularis

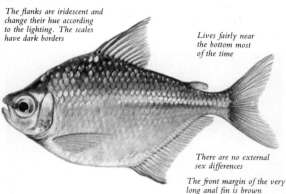

The flanks are iridescent and change their hue according to the lighting. The scales have dark borders

Lives fairly near the bottom most of the time

There are no external sex differences

The front margin of the very long anal fin is brown

The tank should have a dark substrate and it is best to keep the lighting subdued. Each spawning may produce several hundred eggs, which must be protected from their parents. The young grow rapidly and should be given plenty of food. Guyana, Amazon basin, Paraguay. *Length:* to 12 cm; *Diet:* cr, in, wm, vg, dr; *Water:* s, ac, 19–25°C; *Tank:* 60 cm

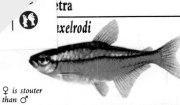

...xelrodi

Iridescent stripe changes colour from green to blue, according to the angle of illumination. The broad red band extends from the mouth to the base of the tail (cp Neon tetra)

♀ is stouter than ♂

This is a lively fish that should be kept in a shoal. It is not easy to breed. Spawning usually takes place in subdued light; soft water (3°DH) is also recommended. Upper Negro. *Length:* to 4 cm; *Diet:* cr, wm, dr; *Water:* s, ac, pt, 23–26°C; *Tank:* 30 cm

Neon tetra

Paracheirodon innesi

♂ is slimmer than ♀. Red extends only from the middle of the body to the base of the tail (cp Cardinal tetra)

Adults are undemanding as regards water composition but soft water (up to 5°DH) is recommended for breeding. The young fishes can gradually be acclimatized to harder water. Upper Amazon. *Length:* to 4 cm; *Diet:* cr, in, wm, vg, dr; *Water:* s, ac, pt, 20–26°C; *Tank:* 30 cm

Black phantom tetra

Megalamphodus megalopterus

♀ *is more colourful than ♂ (an unusual characteristic) and often has reddish fins*

Black shoulder marking is edged with pale mother-of-pearl border

Best kept as a shoal, which will swim near the bottom of the tank most of the time

♂ *has longer, mainly grey or blackish fins*

A relatively recent introduction, this species is quite robust and usually not difficult to breed in soft water (up to 6°DH). Spawning takes place among the plants, preferably in subdued light. Mato Grosso (Brazil). *Length:* to 4 cm; *Diet:* cr, in, wm, dr; *Water:* s, ac, pt, 23–27°C; *Tank:* 40 cm

Red phantom tetra

Megalamphodus sweglesi

Lives in the lower water. Best kept as a shoal

The dorsal fin is longer and more pointed in ♂, usually with a dark blotch; in ♀ it is more variegated and colourful. The ventral fins are usually tipped with white in both sexes

This species is difficult to breed although this may be possible in water no harder than 4°DH. It is less productive than the Black phantom tetra and usually many of the young die. Upper Amazon. *Length:* to 4 cm; *Diet:* cr, in, wm, dr; *Water:* s, ac, pt, 23–27°C; *Tank:* 40 cm

Pink-tailed characin

Chalceus macrolepidotus

Lives near the water surface

An active fish with a tendency to leap out of the water, so the tank must have a good lid. Best kept in a small shoal in a fairly spacious tank, with good illumination. It has a healthy appetite and larger fishes will eat earthworms. The Guianas. *Length:* to 25 cm; *Diet:* cr, in, wm, dr; *Water:* s, 23–27°C; *Tank:* 50 cm

Fanning characin

Pyrrhulina rachoviana

♀

Ventral and anal fins of ♂ are edged with red

The male cleans a spawning site, usually a leaf or a pit in the substrate and then entices the female to spawn by gently nudging her. He fans the eggs with his fins until they hatch (after about 24 hours), which helps to keep them free from infection. R. de la Plata, lower Paraná. *Length:* to 5 cm; *Diet:* cr, in, wm, dr; *Water:* s, ac, pt, 20–28°C; *Tank:* 40 cm

Striped vittata

Pyrrhulina vittata

The male is usually smaller, with reddish to yellowish fins when adult; in the female the fins are more or less colourless. Feeds mostly near the surface. Spawning takes place on a leaf. Not very prolific, usually producing only up to 100 young in a brood. Santarém area (R. Tapajoz, Brazil). *Length:* to 7 cm; *Diet:* cr, in, wm, dr; *Water:* s, ac, pt, 20–28°C; *Tank:* 50 cm

Spraying characin

Copella (= Copeina) arnoldi

Lives in shoals near the surface of the tank

♂ is more colourful; the fins (particularly the dorsal), more pointed

The female leaps out of the water to lay eggs on leaves above the surface (or on the aquarium glass). The male jumps up to fertilize them and keeps them wet by splashing with his tail. After about 30 hours the eggs hatch and the fry drop into the water. The parents should be removed at this stage. The very small fry require tiny live food. R. Pará, lower Amazon. *Length:* to 8 cm; *Diet:* cr, in, wm, dr; *Water:* s, ac, pt, 22–27°C; *Tank:* 40 cm

Red-spotted copeina

Copeina guttata

♂ has yellow fins with orange borders and reddish spots on the flanks; ♀ is smaller, less colourful, with yellowish-grey fins

A hardy fish, which spawns in a small pit in the substrate, the female normally producing large numbers of eggs. Soft water is recommended for breeding, although the eggs have been known to develop in medium-hard water. The tank must have a close-fitting lid as this fish jumps well. Middle Amazon. *Length:* to 15 cm; *Diet:* cr, in, wm, dr; *Water:* s, ac, pt, 22–27°C; *Tank:* 50 cm

Red-eyed characin

Arnoldichthys spilopterus

♂ is brighter, with a more colourful anal fin which may have a red basal spot

Strikingly large scales and greenish iridescence on the flanks

First bred in the aquarium in 1967. The water should not be harder than 3–5°DH for breeding. The male chases the female strenuously during courtship. She lays up to 1,000 eggs which hatch in 30–35 hours. The young are not easy to rear and are susceptible to fish tuberculosis when kept in water which is too hard. Lagos to Niger delta. *Length:* to 7 cm; *Diet:* cr, in, wm, dr; *Water:* s, ac, pt, 24–27°C; *Tank:* 50 cm

Long-finned characin

Alestes longipinnis

The male is larger, with a much elongated dorsal fin. For breeding, which has not often been achieved successfully, it is essential that the water is soft (up to 3°DH). In the wild this species feeds mostly at the surface, taking insects which land on the water. In the aquarium it is unwilling to take food from the bottom. Sierra Leone to Zaïre. *Length:* to 16 cm; *Diet:* cr, in, wm, vg, dr; *Water:* s, ac, pt, 23–26°C; *Tank:* 50 cm

Congo tetra

Micralestes (= Phenacogrammus) interruptus

♂

♂ is larger, its dorsal and anal fins elongated

This species needs plenty of open water for swimming

The elongated rays in the dorsal and caudal fins are particularly well developed in the wild but in fishes bred in captivity these fins are disappointingly short. Spawning often occurs in the morning sun; after a period of strenuous chasing the female produces up to 300 eggs, which hatch within 6 days. The fry can be fed on tiny brine shrimp nauplii and rotifers. Zaïre basin. *Length:* to 12 cm; *Diet:* cr, in, wm, vg, dr; *Water:* s, ac, pt, 23–26°C; *Tank:* 60 cm

Family Anostomidae

Headstanders: found only in tropical America, in slow-flowing waters. Most are small enough for the home aquarium. Some larger species are eaten in their countries of origin.

Three-spot anostomus

Anostomus trimaculatus

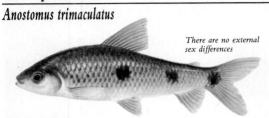

There are no external sex differences

This species has a higher back and is more robust than the Striped anostomus. It requires plenty of vegetable matter in its diet and will also remove algae from the rocks and aquarium glass. The Guianas, lower Amazon. *Length:* to 20 cm; *Diet:* cr, in, wm, vg, dr; *Water:* s, ac, pt, 24–26°C; *Tank:* 60 cm

Striped anostomus

Anostomus anostomus

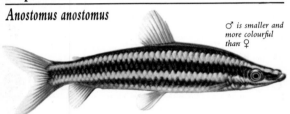

♂ *is smaller and more colourful than* ♀

These fishes are often aggressive towards one another. The mouth is dorsal, so the fish is almost upside-down when browsing on algae growing on leaves or rocks. This species has been bred commercially in aquarium hatcheries but the details are still unknown. Orinoco and Amazon basins, Guyana. *Length:* to 15 cm; *Diet:* cr, in, wm, vg, dr; *Water:* s, ac, pt, 24–26°C; *Tank:* 60 cm

Headstander

Abramites microcephalus (= A. hypselonotus)

The popular name refers to the head-down posture, which also occurs in other members of the family. In the wild this species lives in shoals in fairly shallow water. Large individuals tend to be aggressive towards one another. Guyana, Amazon basin. *Length:* to 12 cm; *Diet:* cr, in, wm, vg, dr; *Water:* s, ac, pt, 24–27°C; *Tank:* 50 cm

Spotted headstander

Chilodus punctatus

An active species, best kept in a tank with a dark substrate and patches of vegetation. As soon as spawning has finished the parent fishes should be transferred from the breeding tank. The eggs hatch in about 4 days and the delicate fry should be fed on brine shrimp nauplii. They assume the head-standing position at a very early stage. North-eastern South America. *Length:* to 12 cm; *Diet:* cr, wm, vg, dr; *Water:* s, ac, pt, 21–27°C; *Tank:* 40 cm

Striped leporinus

Leporinus striatus

Central dark brown stripe is the most conspicuous; the upper and lower ones are paler

In caudal fin of ♂ upper lobe is larger than lower lobe

Members of the genus *Leporinus* have a cleft upper lip: *Leporinus* means 'of a hare'. This species swims mostly in the lower water and will attack soft-leaved plants. The tank must have a lid as this is a keen jumper. Eastern Ecuador, upper Amazon, Mato Grosso (Brazil). *Length:* to 25 cm; *Diet:* cr, in, wm, vg, dr; *Water:* s, ac, pt, 24–26°C; *Tank:* 50 cm

Banded leporinus

Leporinus fasciatus

There are no external sex differences

Varies considerably in colour and pattern

There are usually 9 dark transverse bands in the adults but fewer in the juveniles. They swim with the body in an oblique position, head down, usually in the lower water levels. The diet should be supplemented with plenty of vegetable matter such as boiled lettuce or soaked oatflakes. The tank must have a close-fitting lid. R. Orinoco to R. de la Plata. *Length:* to 30 cm; *Diet:* cr, in, wm, vg, dr; *Water:* s, ac, pt, 24–26°C; *Tank:* 50 cm

Family Hemiodontidae

Pencilfishes: restricted to South America. The lower jaw has no teeth, hence the family name which means 'half-toothed'. There is much disagreement among the experts about the scientific naming of fishes in the genera *Nannostomus* and *Poecilobrycon*.

Golden pencilfish

Nannostomus beckfordi

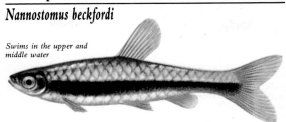

Swims in the upper and middle water

This species has several colour varieties

In some forms ♂ has red on the anal fin and at the base of the caudal fin

Unpolluted rain water may be used for the breeding tank. Spawning usually takes place in the morning; the female lays only a few eggs at each pairing, with a total of about 70–80. The pair must be removed if they start to eat the eggs. Guyana, lower and middle Amazon, R. Negro, R. Paraná. *Length:* to 4.5 cm; *Diet:* cr, in, wm, dr; *Water:* s, ac, pt, 25–27°C; *Tank:* 30 cm

Comma pencilfish

Nannostomus espei

Best kept in a small shoal, this species will swim in the middle water with the body at a slight angle. During the night a transverse bar appears between the two front oblique markings. Mazaruni basin (Guyana). *Length:* to 4 cm; *Diet:* cr, in, wm, dr; *Water:* s, ac, pt, 24–26°C; *Tank:* 30 cm

Dwarf pencilfish

Nannostomus marginatus

These fishes are notorious egg-eaters

Swims in a horizontal position

Anal fin of ♂ is rounded with a black edge; in ♀ it is angular

At night a small dark marking appears on the gill cover and a larger one on the dorsal fin. During spawning periods the eggs can be seen in the female's oviduct (when viewed against the light). Remove the parents immediately after spawning as they will relentlessly attack and eat the eggs which are laid among fine-leaved plants. Western Guyana, Surinam, Amazon basin. *Length:* to 4 cm; *Diet:* cr, in, wm, dr; *Water:* s, ac, pt, 22–26°C; *Tank:* 30 cm

Three-banded pencilfish

Nannostomus trifasciatus

♂ is more slender, more colourful, with a rounded anal fin; ♀ has a straight-cut or concave anal fin

Can be difficult to spawn

Pectoral fins are colourless

This species swims in a horizontal position. During the night the longitudinal stripes become very pale and three broad, dark transverse bands appear on each flank. Spawning often takes place among the roots of floating plants. Western Guyana, Amazon basin. *Length:* to 6 cm; *Diet:* cr, in, wm, dr; *Water:* s, ac, pt, 22–26°C; *Tank:* 30 cm

Tube-mouthed pencilfish

Poecilobrycon eques

The male is slimmer and more colourful with an almost straight belly profile; the female has a distinctly convex belly. Swims head up in an oblique position but rests almost horizontally. At night the body becomes greyish with three broad, dark transverse bands. Middle Amazon, R. Negro. *Length:* to 5 cm; *Diet:* cr, in, wm, dr; *Water:* s, ac, pt, 22–26°C; *Tank:* 30 cm

One-lined pencilfish

Poecilobrycon unifasciatus

In ♂ anal fin has a rounded lower edge; in ♀ it is truncated

♂

As in other pencilfishes the female spawns among the plants. This species swims at an oblique angle with head up, often quite close to the bottom. At night two black markings appear on the flanks. Lower and middle Amazon, R. Negro. *Length:* to 6.5 cm; *Diet:* cr, in, wm, dr; *Water:* s, ac, pt, 23–26°C; *Tank:* 30 cm

Family Citharinidae

Found only in Africa and characterized by the straight lateral line. Small species are suitable for the home aquarium. The young stages of larger species are also suitable but they soon outgrow their tank and the aquarist is faced with the problem of disposal—perhaps to a public aquarium.

One-striped African characin

Nannaethiops unitaeniatus

This is a peaceful fish which does best on a diet of live food. For breeding the tank should have a substrate of clean sand. The eggs, which are laid at random, hatch in 30–40 hours and the fry are free-swimming after a further 5 days. The pair should be removed from the tank as soon as spawning has ceased. West Africa to the White Nile. *Length:* to 7 cm; *Diet:* cr, in, wm, dr; *Water:* s, 22–27°C; *Tank:* 50 cm

Six-banded distichodus

Distichodus sexfasciatus

There are no external sex differences

A shy, peaceful fish which will eventually grow too large for the home aquarium. Provide hiding places by arranging rocks and roots in the tank but do not use plants as the fishes tend to nibble them. Feed on boiled spinach or soaked oatflakes to substitute the plant part of the diet. Lower and middle Zaïre. *Length:* to 25 cm; *Diet:* cr, in, wm, vg, dr; *Water:* s, 24–26°C; *Tank:* 50 cm

Pike characin

Phago maculatus

In the wild this fish feeds mainly on small fishes, so it is not a candidate for a community tank. Its appearance and feeding habits are very pike-like. It is a shy fish, best kept in subdued light, in a tank planted with vegetation and pieces of well-washed root to provide shelter. Niger basin. *Length:* to 14 cm; *Diet:* in, fh; *Water:* nc, 26–28°C; *Tank:* 30 cm

African redfin

Neolebias ansorgii

At spawning time the male has blood-red fins (except the pectorals) and the eggs may be seen in the oviduct of the female (when viewed against the light). The female lays about 200 eggs in batches which hatch within 40 hours and the fry are free-swimming after 5 days. They are not easy to rear and require infusorians or nauplii at first. Central Africa. *Length:* to 10 cm; *Diet:* cr, in, wm, dr; *Water:* s. 23–28°C; *Tank:* 50 cm

Family Gasteropelecidae

Hatchetfishes: found only in tropical America. The distinguishing characteristic of this family is the prominent breast region that encloses an enlarged shoulder-girdle to which the muscles of the pectoral fins are attached. By rapidly beating these fins the fish is able to glide over the surface of the water for short distances (about three metres). Only a few species have bred in captivity. Hatchetfishes are best kept in a tank where the other fishes live in the middle and lower water. They are very susceptible to white spot.

Common hatchetfish

Gasteropelecus sternicla

Lives near the surface of the water

The body is silvery in reflected light

♂ is smaller than ♀

This species has only been bred in the aquarium on a few occasions. Failure to breed may be due to a lack of understanding of the conditions required. It is likely that water hardness plays an important part: the water should be very soft (2–4°DH). Guyana, Surinam, Peru, middle and lower Amazon. *Length:* to 6.5 cm; *Diet:* cr, in, wm, dr; *Water:* s, ac, pt, 23–29°C; *Tank:* 50 cm

Silver hatchetfish

Gasteropelecus levis

Pectoral fins are used for gliding over the surface of the water

Sometimes has a dark marking at the base of the dorsal fin

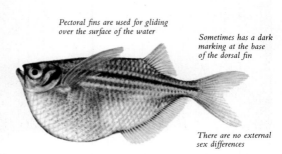

There are no external sex differences

It can sometimes be difficult to distinguish this species from *G. sternicla*. The Silver hatchetfish is rather more delicate. Both are apt to leap out of the water, so the tank must have a close-fitting lid. Lower Amazon. *Length:* to 6 cm; *Diet:* cr, in, wm, dr; *Water:* s, ac, pt, 24–29°C; *Tank:* 50 cm

Black-winged hatchetfish

Carnegiella marthae

This species is difficult to breed, even in very soft water (2–5°DH). The female lays batches of 2–5 eggs just below the surface of the water and these hatch in 30–35 hours. The young start to become hatchet-shaped after about 20 days. Orinoco and Amazon basins. *Length:* to 3.5 cm; *Diet:* cr, in, dr; *Water:* s, ac, pt, 23–29°C; *Tank:* 40 cm

Marbled hatchetfish

Carnegiella strigata

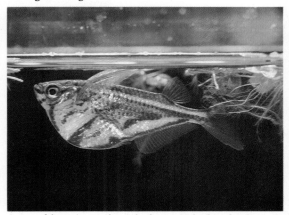

A peaceful species, perhaps the best-suited of its family to the aquarium, but it is not often bred. Like *C. marthae* the female spawns near the surface among fine-leaved plants. Light should be prevented from entering the tank from the sides as this disturbs the fishes. Guyana, lower and middle Amazon. *Length:* to 4.5 cm; *Diet:* cr, in, dr; *Water:* s, ac, pt, 24–29°C; *Tank:* 40 cm

Family Cyprinidae

The carps and barbs: a large family with species in all parts of the world except Australia and South America. They never have an adipose fin. In most the mouth is protruding and some species have one or two pairs of barbels at the corners of the mouth. There are no teeth on the jaws but there are teeth on the floor of the pharynx. Most of the species suitable for the aquarium are tropical but there are also cold-water species such as the Goldfish, Golden orfe, Minnow and Bitterling. For these temperate fishes, care should be taken that the water does not become overheated in warm weather; good aeration is essential.

Goldfish

O **Pa** ⊜ ✦ ✓

Carassius auratus

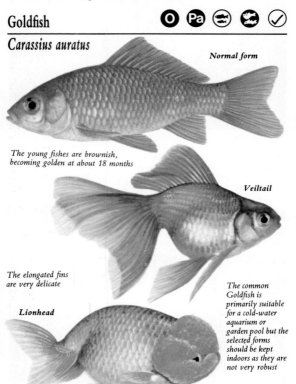

Normal form

The young fishes are brownish, becoming golden at about 18 months

Veiltail

The elongated fins are very delicate

Lionhead

The common Goldfish is primarily suitable for a cold-water aquarium or garden pool but the selected forms should be kept indoors as they are not very robust

First brought to Portugal *c.*1611, this fast-growing fish has been bred and selected in the Far East over a long period of time producing domesticated forms such as the Veiltail, Lionhead, Telescope-eye and Oranda. Under good conditions the ordinary Goldfish lives for 20–25 years; the selected forms survive for a shorter period. Breeding is not difficult; the eggs hatch in about 7 days and the fry hang from the plants for a few days, consuming the yolk sac contents. They can then be fed on fine dried food. The western subspecies is known as the Prussian carp. Originally China to eastern Europe, but introduced to many other parts of the world. *Length:* to 20 cm; *Diet:* cr, in, wm, vg, dr; *Water:* nc, 4–24°C; *Tank:* 50 cm

Golden orfe

Leisciscus idus

♂ *is smaller, with white tubercles at spawning time*

This is the golden variety of the Ide or Silver orfe. It is only suitable for the home aquarium when quite small but is a good pond fish—in fact many think it superior in appearance to the Goldfish. A cold-water species. Spawns from April to July. Europe north of the Pyrenees to western Siberia. *Length:* to 75 cm; *Diet:* cr, in, wm, vg, dr; *Water:* nc, 4–20°C; *Tank:* 60 cm

Minnow

Phoxinus phoxinus

Lives in shoals in the upper water

♂ *is slimmer*

A cold-water species

Spawns from April to July. They are not difficult to breed in an unheated tank, with water no deeper than 15 cm. The eggs are usually laid on stones and they hatch in about 6 days. Feed the fry on tiny crustaceans at first. Europe (except southern Spain and Iceland) eastwards into USSR. *Length:* to 14 cm; *Diet:* cr, in, wm, dr; *Water:* nc, 4–20°C; *Tank:* 60 cm

Rhodeus sericeus

A cold-water species

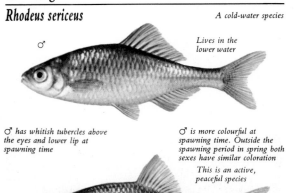

♂

*Lives in the
lower water*

*♂ has whitish tubercles above
the eyes and lower lip at
spawning time*

*♂ is more colourful at
spawning time. Outside the
spawning period in spring both
sexes have similar coloration*

*This is an active,
peaceful species*

*♀ has a pink ovipositor c. 45 mm
long projecting from the anal fin*

♀

The eggs are laid in a Swan mussel (*Anodonta*). Before spawning
the female touches the shell repeatedly with her mouth, which
evidently accustoms the mollusc to egg-laying so that it does not
close its valves while the ovipositor is inserted and the eggs are
laid. The male sheds sperm over the mollusc to fertilize the eggs,
which hatch and remain as fry inside the mussel for 4–5 weeks.
Once they have emerged they can be fed on very fine food. This
unusual mode of reproduction can be observed in the aquarium.
Central Europe, introduced into Britain. *Length:* to 9 cm; *Diet:* cr,
in, wm, dr; *Water:* nc, 4–22°C; *Tank:* 50 cm

White Cloud Mountain minnow

Tanichthys albonubes

♂ *is smaller and
more slender*

*Lives in the
upper water*

A cold-water species

This species can survive in a temperature of 16°C in winter . They spawn on fine-leaved plants and the eggs hatch in about 48 hours. Feed the fry on very tiny live food and some dried food. The parents may eat the eggs. White Cloud Mountain (Kuang-chou). *Length:* to 6 cm; *Diet:* cr, wm, dr; *Water:* nc, 18–22°C; *Tank:* 30 cm

Pearl danio

Brachydanio albolineatus

♂ *is smaller
and slimmer*

*Lives in the upper
and middle water*

*Two pairs of barbels:
the lower pair very long*

*Sunlight encourages
activity and brings out
brighter colours*

One of the easiest aquarium fishes to keep and breed. Allow a female to settle into the breeding tank. About 48 hours later (in the evening) put in two males. Next morning she will spawn with one of the males and lay large numbers of eggs which hatch in 20–24 hours. The fry live on the yolk sac contents at first and can then be given tiny live food. South-east Asia. *Length:* to 5.5 cm; *Diet:* cr, wm, dr; *Water:* nc, 20–25°C; *Tank:* 40 cm

Zebra danio

Brachydanio rerio

Gill cover has bluish markings

♂ *is smaller and more slender than* ♀

Two pairs of barbels

An excellent fish for the beginner as it has no special requirements. Spawning takes place as in the Pearl danio. The parents
should be removed after spawning as they may attack the eggs.
Some aquarists feed the fishes on whiteworms while they are
spawning which possibly distracts their attention from the brood.
Eastern India. *Length:* to 4.5 cm; *Diet:* cr, wm, dr; *Water:* nc, 19–
25°C; *Tank:* 30 cm

Bengal danio

Danio devario

*Mouth faces upwards.
There are no barbels
in this species*

*Lives in the upper water.
Best kept as a shoal*

♂ *is slimmer and
more colourful*

Even for breeding the water composition is not important.
Suitable spawning sites may be provided by clumps of *Cabomba*
(p 8) or other fine-leaved plants which need not necessarily be
growing in the substrate but can be anchored with a small rock.
Spawning and rearing as for the Pearl danio. A good breeding
pair will often mate again after 3 or 4 weeks and they are very
prolific. The young grow rapidly. Pakistan, eastern India,
Bangladesh. *Length:* to 10 cm; *Diet:* cr, in, wm, dr; *Water:* nc, 21–
24°C; *Tank:* 50 cm

Giant danio

Danio malabaricus

The central blue stripe is straight in the ♂; in the ♀ it curves upwards at the tail base

♂ is more slender

♂

One pair of barbels

For breeding the water temperature should be raised to 25–28°C. Like many others, this fish becomes sexually mature at a length of approximately 6 cm, so it is very suitable for the home aquarium. It can be bred in the same way as the Pearl danio. Best kept as a small shoal, this is an active species which lives in the upper water. Western coastal areas of India and Sri Lanka. *Length:* to 12 cm; *Diet:* cr, in, wm, dr; *Water:* nc, 20–24°C; *Tank:* 50 cm

Flying fox

Epalzeorhynchus kallopterus

The mouth is directed downwards with a fringed upper lip. There are two pairs of barbels

This attractive fish is rather intolerant towards others of its own species so the tank should be large enough for each individual to set up its own territory. Although it has not yet been bred in captivity, this is a useful fish as it grazes on algae growing on the rocks and also removes the planarians which sometimes infest tanks in large numbers. Borneo, Sumatra. *Length:* to 12 cm; *Diet:* cr, in, wm, vg, dr; *Water:* s, 22–25°C; *Tank:* 50 cm

Red-tailed labeo

Labeo bicolor

Also known by the misleading name Red-tailed black 'shark'

♂ is more slender

Two pairs of barbels

Best kept in subdued light, in a tank arranged with rocks providing one or two hiding places. This species has not been bred very often. In one successful attempt an aquarist used water at pH 6.8; a small number of eggs hatched in 30–60 hours and the young were silvery-grey until they were about 8 mm long. Thailand. *Length:* to 12 cm; *Diet:* cr, in, wm, vg, dr; *Water:* s, ac, pt, 22–26°C; *Tank:* 50 cm

Black labeo

Morulius chrysophekadion

There are no external sex differences

Two pairs of barbels

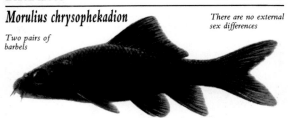

This fish is rather too large for the home aquarium but it makes a splendid exhibit in a public aquarium. It is useful as a tank 'vacuum cleaner' as it sucks algae off the tank glass, rocks and plants. It is often known by the misleading name Black 'shark'. *Length:* to 60 cm; *Diet:* cr, in, wm, vg, dr; *Water:* s, ac, pt, 22–27°C; *Tank:* 60 cm

Arulius barb

Barbus arulius

♂ has elongated dorsal fin rays

Inhabits the middle and lower water

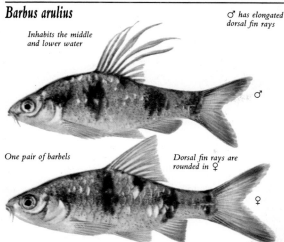

♂

One pair of barbels

Dorsal fin rays are rounded in ♀

♀

Although the quality of the water is not critical, breeding is usually more successful in old or mature water which has had plants growing in it. The broods are not large (up to 100 eggs). South-east India. *Length:* to 12 cm; *Diet:* cr, in, wm, vg, dr; *Water:* nc, 24–26°C; *Tank:* 60 cm

Orange barb

Barbus barilioides

A lively fish best kept as a small shoal in a tank with subdued light and preferably a dark substrate. Clumps of plants should be provided to give shelter for this rather shy species which lives in the middle and lower water. The dorsal fin has a large, sometimes indistinct red marking near the front edge. There is one pair of relatively large barbels. Southern Africa. *Length:* to 5 cm; *Diet:* cr, in, wm, vg, dr; *Water:* nc, 23–25°C; *Tank:* 40 cm

Swamp barb

Barbus chola

When in good condition the red colour on the gill cover is quite prominent

At spawning time fins are reddish in the ♂ and yellowish in the ♀

One pair of short barbels

♂ is smaller

In the wild this fish is often found in paddy-fields. It is a very undemanding species, particularly as regards temperature, and can be kept at 18–20°C during the winter. Breeding is not difficult, although soft water is recommended. The eggs are scattered at random among the vegetation. Eastern India, Burma. *Length:* to 15 cm; *Diet:* cr, in, wm, vg, dr; *Water:* nc, 23–25°C; *Tank:* 50 cm

Rosy barb

Barbus conchonius

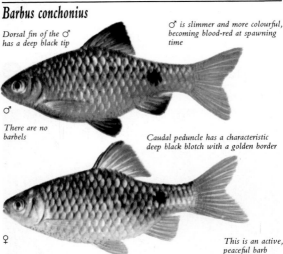

Dorsal fin of the ♂ has a deep black tip

♂ is slimmer and more colourful, becoming blood-red at spawning time

♂

There are no barbels

Caudal peduncle has a characteristic deep black blotch with a golden border

♀

This is an active, peaceful barb

The female is often the more active partner during the boisterous courtship. Spawning usually takes place among dense vegetation. To prevent the eggs from being eaten by the parents the substrate should have a top layer of gravel into which they can sink. Alternatively, the parents can be removed after spawning. The eggs hatch in 20–24 hours (at 23–25°C). The fry lie on the bottom at first but soon attach themselves to the plants or rise to the surface. After consuming the yolk sac contents they can be fed on tiny live food such as rotifers. North-eastern India. *Length:* to 14 cm; *Diet:* cr, in, wm, vg, dr; *Water:* nc, 20–25°C; *Tank:* 60 cm

Cuming's barb

Barbus cumingi

*Fins vary in colour
from red to yellow*

*♂ is smaller and slimmer,
with more brightly coloured
fins*

*There are no
barbels*

*Swims in the middle
and lower water*

The coloration is enhanced when this species is kept as a small shoal. It can be bred like the Rosy barb but at a slightly higher temperature. Lives in mountain streams in the wild. Sri Lanka. *Length:* to 5 cm; *Diet:* cr, in, wm, vg, dr; *Water:* nc, 24–27°C; *Tank:* 40 cm

Clown barb

Barbus everetti

*Keep only with other
species of the same size*

♂ is smaller

Two pairs of barbels

For breeding, soft neutral water is usually recommended. The breeding pair should be kept apart for some weeks and fed a varied diet, including plant matter (such as boiled lettuce). They spawn in the early morning sunshine, preferably among clumps of fine-leaved plants. This is one of the barbs prone to eating the leaves of the plants. Singapore, Borneo, Sarawak, Bunguran Island. *Length:* to 10 cm; *Diet:* cr, in, wm, vg, dr; *Water:* s, 25–27°C; *Tank:* 50 cm

Striped barb

Barbus fasciatus

♂ is smaller than ♀

Usually grows to only 6 cm in the aquarium

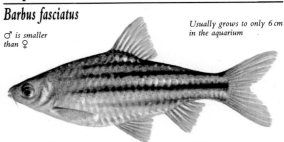

Two pairs of barbels

♀ has less prominent stripes on the flanks

Although quite happy in a community tank, this species is often said to live better when kept as a small shoal without other species. For breeding the water temperature should be raised to 26–28°C. The female spawns at random among the plants. The similarly striped Lined barb *B. lineatus* from Johore, Malaya, has no barbels. Borneo, Sumatra, Malaya. *Length:* 10 cm; *Diet:* cr, in, wm, vg, dr; *Water:* nc, 21–26°C; *Tank:* 50 cm

Golden dwarf barb

Barbus gelius

There are no barbels

♂ is more slender than ♀

This is a very undemanding fish which will breed even at the relatively low temperature of 22°C and can be kept during the winter at 16–18°C. The eggs adhere to the vegetation and hatch in about 25 hours. At first the fry hang from the leaves and can later be fed on rotifers and on finely powdered dried food. Central India, Bangladesh. *Length:* to 4 cm; *Diet:* cr, in; *Water:* nc, 20–22°C; *Tank:* 40 cm

Spanner barb

Barbus lateristriga

♂ is more slender

Base of dorsal fin is deep red in the ♂

Two pairs of barbels

Lives mainly near the bottom

A slow-swimming fish, suitable for a tank which can accommodate larger species, although even in a large tank it will not reach the length recorded in the wild. It is very prolific. The eggs are spawned among the plants and care must be taken as the parents may sometimes attack their own eggs. Malay Peninsula, Indonesia. *Length:* to 18 cm; *Diet:* cr, in, wm, vg, dr; *Water:* s, ac, 20–25°C; *Tank:* 60 cm

Black ruby

Barbus nigrofasciatus

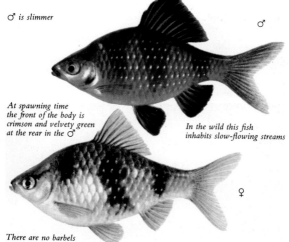

♂ is slimmer

♂

At spawning time the front of the body is crimson and velvety green at the rear in the ♂

In the wild this fish inhabits slow-flowing streams

♀

There are no barbels

A popular and prolific species, which usually spawns in the morning sunshine. For breeding the temperature should be kept at 26–28°C and the tank should have some floating plants. When not breeding the male is yellowish-grey with 3 or 4 somewhat indistinct transverse bars; these bars appear as blotches in the female. Sri Lanka. *Length:* to 6 cm; *Diet:* cr, in, wm, vg, dr; *Water:* nc, 24–28°C; *Tank:* 50 cm

Island barb

Barbus oligolepis

The relatively large scales give the flanks a net-like appearance, hence the alternative popular name of Checker barb. The dorsal and anal fins are red with black edges in the male, yellowish and with less prominent dark edges in the female. There is one pair of barbels. It is not a difficult fish to breed and should be kept in a small shoal. Sumatra. *Length:* to 5 cm; *Diet:* cr, in, wm, vg, dr; *Water:* s, ac, 21–25°C; *Tank:* 30 cm

Dwarf barb

Barbus phutunio

♂ *is slimmer, with more conspicuous flank markings than the female*

The back becomes somewhat tall in older individuals

There are no barbels

Compared to other barbs this is not a prolific fish; the female usually lays only 60–80 eggs. It is easy to keep, even in a small tank which should have clumps of vegetation round the edges and sufficient open water for swimming. Sri Lanka, eastern India, Bangladesh. *Length:* to 8 cm; *Diet:* cr, in, wm, vg, dr; *Water:* s, 21–25°C; *Tank:* 30 cm

Schwanenfeld's barb

Barbus schwanenfeldi

The back becomes high, particularly in older specimens

Also called the Tinfoil barb

There are no external sex differences

Two pairs of barbels

This is a good fish for the home aquarium when less than about 7 cm but it grows very rapidly and will soon outstay its welcome, becoming more suitable as an exhibit in a public aquarium. It must be given plenty of plant food to prevent it attacking the plants. South-east Asia. *Length:* to 32 cm; *Diet:* cr, in, wm, vg, dr; *Water:* nc, 20–25°C; *Tank:* 70 cm

Green barb

Barbus semifasciolatus

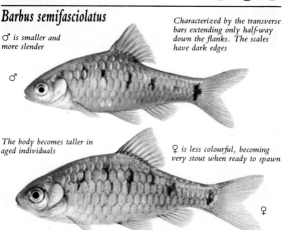

♂ is smaller and more slender

Characterized by the transverse bars extending only half-way down the flanks. The scales have dark edges

The body becomes taller in aged individuals

♀ is less colourful, becoming very stout when ready to spawn

One pair of very small barbels

This peaceful, hardy species lives in the middle and lower water. Best kept as a shoal

A relatively dull-looking fish, although the boisterous preliminaries to spawning make it an interesting addition to the aquarium. The male circles the female repeatedly, sometimes touching her with his snout or beating her with his tail trying to move her into the vegetation. The yellowish eggs hatch in about 24 hours. Also known as the Chinese or Half-striped barb. South-east China. *Length:* to 7 cm; *Diet:* cr, in, wm, vg, dr; *Water:* s, ac, 19–25°C; *Tank:* 40 cm

Golden barb

Barbus 'schuberti'

Swims in the upper
and middle water

♂ has dark spots
on the flanks

The name *'schuberti'* is not scientifically valid. It has been suggested that this is a selected form of *B. semifasciolatus*. It is a good fish for the home aquarium and will breed more readily than the Green barb. Origin unknown. *Length:* to 7 cm; *Diet:* cr, in, wm, vg, dr; *Water:* nc, 20–25°C; *Tank:* 40 cm

Stoliczka's barb

Barbus stoliczkanus

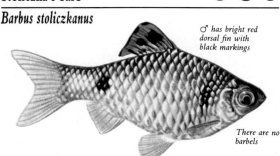

♂ has bright red
dorsal fin with
black markings

There are no
barbels

The eggs are scattered at random and most fall to the bottom. They hatch in about 35 hours and the fry are free-swimming some 48 hours later. Some authorities regard this as a subspecies of the Two-spot barb *B. ticto* which occurs in Sri Lanka and has a more slender outline. Lower Irrawaddy (Burma). *Length:* to 6 cm; *Diet:* cr, in, wm, vg, dr; *Water:* nc, 19–25°C; *Tank:* 40 cm

Sumatra barb

Barbus tetrazona tetrazona

The flanks are iridescent yellow with 4 black transverse bars, the third extending to the dorsal and anal fins

Lives in the midwater

♂ is smaller and redder

There are no barbels

Also known as the Tiger barb. The breeding pair is sometimes fed on whiteworms while spawning to prevent the eggs from being eaten. The female may produce 500–1,000 eggs at a time and these hatch in 24–30 hours. The adults tend to nibble the fins of Angelfishes. Sumatra, Borneo. *Length:* to 7 cm; *Diet:* cr, in, wm, vg, dr; *Water:* nc, 20–25°C; *Tank:* 40 cm

Banded barb

Barbus tetrazona partipentazona

♂ is more slender

An active barb which lives in the midwater

A subspecies of the Sumatra barb, distinguished by having an extra transverse bar extending from the dorsal fin to halfway down the flank. Breed in the same way as the Sumatra barb. Kampochea, south-east Thailand. *Length:* to 6 cm; *Diet:* cr, in, wm, vg, dr; *Water:* nc, 20–25°C; *Tank:* 40 cm

Cherry barb

Barbus titteya

Lives in the middle water

♂

♂ is more colourful and very red at spawning time

♂s may spar with one another but not seriously

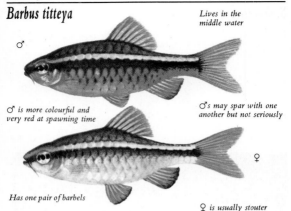

Has one pair of barbels

♀

♀ is usually stouter

This rather shy species does best in a tank with subdued lighting and plenty of plants to provide hiding places. The female produces 200–250 eggs at a time which hatch in about 25 hours. The parents should be fed on whiteworms during spawning. Small rivers in Sri Lanka. *Length:* to 5 cm; *Diet:* cr, in, wm, vg, dr; *Water:* nc, 23–26°C; *Tank:* 30 cm

Red-tailed rasbora

Rasbora borapetensis

A very prolific species

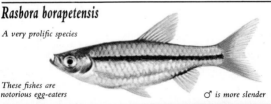

These fishes are notorious egg-eaters

♂ is more slender

The breeding tank should not have a substrate as the young are sensitive to impurities in the water. However, dense clumps of fine-leaved plants should be provided to protect the eggs from their parents. Thailand. *Length:* to 5 cm; *Diet:* cr, in, wm, dr; *Water:* s, ac, pt, 21–26°C; *Tank:* 40 cm

Slender rasbora

Rasbora daniconius

This is a prolific species, hence the need for a relatively large tank.
As soon as the fry are free-swimming they should be fed on
newly hatched brine shrimp larvae. Sri Lanka, south-east India,
Burma, Thailand. *Length:* to 10 cm; *Diet:* cr, in, wm, dr; *Water:* s,
24–26°C; *Tank:* 60 cm

Eye-spot rasbora

Rasbora dorsiocellata dorsiocellata

*The large black spot with
a pale border on the dorsal
fin is characteristic. The
caudal fin is reddish in the
♂ and yellowish in the ♀*

The female lays numerous eggs on the upperside of large leaves.
The eyes are rather yellow; in the related *R. dorsiocellata macro-
phthalma* the eyes are larger with blue-green iridescence below.
Malaya, Sumatra. *Length:* to 6.5 cm; *Diet:* cr, in, wm, dr; *Water:*
s, ac, 24–26°C; *Tank:* 40 cm

Harlequin fish

Rasbora heteromorpha

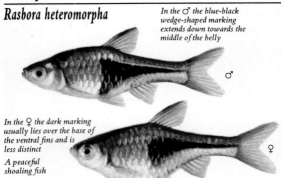

In the ♂ the blue-black wedge-shaped marking extends down towards the middle of the belly

♂

In the ♀ the dark marking usually lies over the base of the ventral fins and is less distinct

A peaceful shoaling fish

♀

The female spawns on the underside of leaves such as *Crypto-coryne* (p 8) usually at a temperature of 26–28°C. This whole process takes two or three hours and yields up to 250 eggs. South Thailand, Malaya, Sumatra. *Length:* to 4.5 cm; *Diet:* cr, wm, in, dr; *Water:* s, ac, pt, 22–25°C; *Tank:* 30 cm

Spotted rasbora

Rasbora maculata

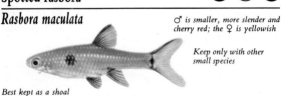

♂ is smaller, more slender and cherry red; the ♀ is yellowish

Keep only with other small species

Best kept as a shoal

The tank should have a dark (preferably peat) substrate. To encourage spawning the pair should be separated and fed well for about two weeks. They can then be united in a tank on their own, in water at 26–28°C. Not a very prolific species. Southern Malaya, Singapore, Sumatra. *Length:* to 2.5 cm; *Diet:* cr, wm, dr; *Water:* s, ac, pt, 21–25°C; *Tank:* 30 cm

Red-striped rasbora

Rasbora pauciperforata

This species is best bred in a tank without a substrate and a few anchored clumps of fine-leaved plants. Those eggs that escape the attention of the parents hatch in 26–30 hours and the fry are free-swimming 3–5 days later. Feed them on rotifers at first and later on brine shrimp nauplii. Malaya, Sumatra. *Length:* to 7 cm; *Diet:* cr, wm, dr; *Water:* s, ac, pt, 21–26°C; *Tank:* 30 cm

Scissors-tail

Rasbora trilineata

The popular name refers to the scissor-like movement of the two lobes of the caudal fin. For breeding the water should be no harder than 10–12°DH. The fishes spawn at random in the water. Malaya, Borneo, Sumatra. *Length:* to 15 cm; *Diet:* cr, in, wm, dr; *Water:* s, ac, pt, 18–25°C; *Tank:* 50 cm

Pearly rasbora

Rasbora vaterifloris

♂ is more slender, with orange or reddish fins; ♀ has yellowish fins

♂

This species should be kept in subdued lighting and the tank can be quite small. Breeding should be attempted in a clean, bare tank with a few clumps of fine-leaved plants. These fishes are bad egg-eaters. Sri Lanka. *Length:* to 4 cm; *Diet:* cr, wm, dr; *Water:* s, ac, pt, 24–26°C; *Tank:* 40 cm

Family Gyrinocheilidae

Only three species, living in streams in south-east Asia. They feed by rasping algae with the ridges of the suctorial mouth.

Indian algae-eater

Gyrinocheilus aymonieri

While sucking algae it cannot take in water for respiration through the mouth. Instead, water enters the gill chamber through a hole in the upper part of the gill slit

♂ is smaller

The mouth faces downwards with thick, folded lips forming a suction device

Sometimes known as the Sucker loach, this is one of the best removers of algae from the aquarium. Becomes aggressive with age, so keep only one in a community tank. Thailand. *Length:* to 25 cm; *Diet:* vg, dr; *Water:* nc, 20–30°C; *Tank:* 40 cm

Family Cobitidae

Loaches: found in Europe and Asia., They can surviv___
poor in oxygen by taking in air at the surface and pass___
the alimentary canal to the hind gut where the ___
extracted. They have a spine beneath each eye whi___ ___n be
erected, creating a hazard to predators trying to swallow the fish.

Coolie loach

Acanthophthalmus sp.

Half-banded coolie loach
Acanthophthalmus semicinctus

Lives on the bottom
of the tank

Second pectoral fin ray
is thicker in the ♂

Three pairs of barbels

The photograph shows one of the many different forms of the
Coolie loach. They breed very rarely in captivity and accounts of
what happens do not all agree. It is most likely that the fishes coil
around one another near the surface and shed sperm and eggs into
the water. Malaya. *Length:* to 8 cm; *Diet:* wm, vg, dr; *Water:* s,
24–30°C; *Tank:* 30 cm

Long-nosed loach

Acanthopsis choirorhynchus

There are three pairs
of short barbels

No external sex
differences

The small mouth faces downwards, the lower lip is fringed.
Borneo, Sumatra, Java. *Length:* to 18 cm; *Diet:* cr, in, wm, dr;
Water: s, 25–28°C; *Tank:* 30 cm

Botia horae

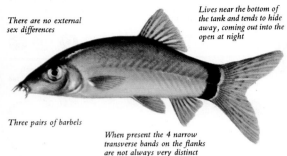

There are no external sex differences

Lives near the bottom of the tank and tends to hide away, coming out into the open at night

Three pairs of barbels

When present the 4 narrow transverse bands on the flanks are not always very distinct

Widely distributed in Thailand but still nothing is known about the breeding habits of this loach. The main characteristic feature is the dorsal fin which is made up of only 8 soft rays and positioned directly above the ventral fins as in some other species of *Botia*. Thailand. *Length:* to 10 cm; *Diet:* cr, in, wm, vg, dr; *Water:* s, 26–30°C; *Tank:* 30 cm

Banded loach

Botia hymenophysa

The two-pointed spine in front of the eye is about as long as the diameter of the eye

There are no external sex differences

Three pairs of barbels

The flanks are usually clearly marked with about 11 transverse bands

A shy species which should be kept in a tank with a soft substrate in which, like other loaches, it spends much time burrowing for worms and insect larvae. Thailand, Malay Peninsula, Borneo, Sumatra, Java. *Length:* to 21 cm; *Diet:* cr, in, wm, dr; *Water:* s, 24–30°C; *Tank:* 30 cm

Clown loach

Botia macracantha

This is the most brightly coloured member of the genus

Has 4 pairs of barbels

There are no external sex differences

This loach often lives for many years in the aquarium but will never reach its full length in captivity. It is also possible that it does not reach sexual maturity, which would explain the lack of success in breeding. This species is sensitive to chemicals in the water. Borneo, Sumatra. *Length:* to 30 cm; *Diet:* cr, wm, vg, dr; *Water:* s, 24–30°C; *Tank:* 50 cm

Orange-finned loach

Botia modesta

There is usually an indistinct marking on the caudal peduncle

Three pairs of barbels

There are no external sex differences

A shy species which is usually more active at night. As in the other loaches the barbels act as tactile organs and play an important part in the location of prey, such as insect larvae and worms living in or on the substrate. Thailand, Vietnam, Malaya. *Length:* to 10 cm; *Diet:* cr, in, wm, dr; *Water:* s, 24–30°C; *Tank:* 30 cm

Dwarf loach

Botia sidthimunki

There are three pairs of barbels

No external sex differences

This small species usually spends more time swimming in open water than the other loaches. It is active and best kept in a small shoal; solitary individuals do not thrive in captivity. Feed mainly on live food. Thailand. *Length:* to 3.5 cm; *Diet:* cr, in, wm, vg, dr; *Water:* s, 24–30°C; *Tank:* 30 cm

Family Electrophoridae

Found in South America. Modified muscles produce electric pulses varying in strength to suit different purposes.

Electric eel

Electrophorus electricus

Too large for the home aquarium. A mainly nocturnal fish with electric organs along the flanks which send out electric pulses; some are used for stunning prey (up to 300 volts), others for navigation, particularly at night and in muddy water. Middle and lower Amazon, north-eastern South America. *Length:* to 230 cm; *Diet:* wm, fh, mt; *Water:* nc, 23–28°C; *Tank:* 100 cm

Family Gymnotidae

A small family found only in South America. The species have no ventral fins. Weak electric pulses help them to navigate.

Banded knifefish

Gymnotus carapo

The tank should be kept fairly dark, with roots and rocks to provide shelter during the day. The fish emerges to search for food at night using the small electric organs for orientation. Undulations of the long anal fin enable it to move backwards and forwards. Guatemala to R. de la Plata. *Length:* to 60 cm; *Diet:* in, wm, fh, mt, vg, dr; *Water:* s, 22–28°C; *Tank:* 100 cm

Family Siluridae

Restricted to the Old World, these naked catfishes (with no scales or bony plates) have 1–6 pairs of long barbels, no adipose fin and a long anal fin. The dorsal and ventral fins are tiny or absent.

Glass catfish

Kryptopterus bicirrhis

In spite of their fragile appearance these are hardy fishes. Best kept as a small shoal in a well-planted tank with peaceful occupants. They spend most of their time in the midwater with the body in an oblique position, their tails flickering constantly. Borneo, Sumatra, Java. *Length:* to 10 cm; *Diet:* cr, in, wm, dr; *Water:* nc, 20–26°C; *Tank:* 40 cm

Family Schilbeidae

Restricted to the Old World. These catfishes have an elongated body, 2–4 pairs of barbels and a long anal fin. The dorsal fin is short and its first ray is spiny.

African glass catfish

Eutropiellus debauwi

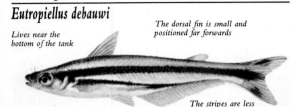

The dorsal fin is small and positioned far forwards

Lives near the bottom of the tank

Three pairs of barbels

The stripes are less pronounced in the ♀

A very lively species best kept as a shoal in a tank with plenty of space for swimming as it moves about continuously. The first spine of the pectoral and dorsal fins is sharp and may get caught up in the net. Malebo Pool (Stanley Pool), (Zaïre). *Length:* to 8 cm; *Diet:* cr, in, wm, dr; *Water:* s, ac, 24–26°C; *Tank:* 50 cm

Family Clariidae

Found in Africa, Madagascar, Malaysia and The Philippines, these are naked catfishes which have 4 pairs of barbels. Some species spend the dry season buried in mud.

Clarias catfish

Clarias batrachus

Survives in waters deficient in oxygen by using its accessory air-breathing organs to take in air at the surface. In the wild this enables it to come out on land at night and search for food. There is an albino form of this species. Eastern India, Burma, Malay Archipelago. *Length:* to 55 cm; *Diet:* in, wm, fh, mt, dr; *Water:* s, 20–25°C; *Tank:* 100 cm

Family Mochocidae

Restricted to Africa south of the Sahara, these [...]
There is one pair of barbels on the upper j[...]
lower jaw. Some species have a long adipos[...]

Family Pim

Found onl[...]
These a[...]
barbel[...]

Angel catfish

Synodontis angelicus

A hardy, lively fish best kept in a dimly lit tank as it tends to hide from bright light. Markings are more pronounced in young specimens. This is an uncommon species that is not often available on the market. West Africa. *Length:* to 20 cm; *Diet:* cr, in, wm, vg, dr; *Water:* s, 22–27°C; *Tank:* 50 cm

Upside-down catfish

Synodontis nigriventris

♂ has a row of spots at the back of the head; these are lacking in the ♀

Swims and feeds upside-down

May nibble the fins of smaller fishes

This species has rarely been bred in captivity. In one case small clumps of eggs were laid in a dark corner of the tank attached to the glass. They hatched in 7–8 days. At first the fry swam in the normal way but after 7–10 weeks they started to swim upside-down. Zaïre. *Length:* to 9 cm; *Diet:* cr, in, vg, dr; *Water:* nc, 22–27°C; *Tank:* 60 cm

...elodidae

...y in southern Mexico, Central and South America. ...e elongated naked catfishes, usually with three pairs of ...s and an adipose fin.

...potted pimelodella

Pimelodella picta

This is a peaceful, mainly nocturnal catfish, so it is best kept in subdued light. It has the useful habit of scavenging odd scraps of food. Venezuela to R. de la Plata. *Length:* to 17 cm; *Diet:* in, wm; *Water:* s, 18–24°C; *Tank:* 50 cm

Family Callichthyidae

Armoured catfishes: restricted to Trinidad and South America. They have smooth, overlapping bony plates in two rows along each flank, an adipose fin and a variable number of barbels.

Armoured catfish

Callichthys callichthys

Moves out at night in search of prey

♂ *is more colourful, with a thicker first pectoral fin ray*

A mainly nocturnal species. The parents build a nest of bubbles under broad leaves, in which the female lays 100–200 eggs. The male can be heard to grunt loudly while he is guarding the nest. The eggs hatch in 4–5 days. Eastern Brazil to R. de la Plata. *Length:* to 18 cm; *Diet:* in, fh, vg, dr; *Water:* nc, 18–26°C; *Tank:* 50 cm

Genus *Corydoras*

All the species of *Corydoras* are useful to have in a community tank as they keep the substrate clean and do not interfere in any way with other species swimming above them.

While tolerant as regards tank conditions they react adversely to being disturbed. They do best in a tank with a sandy substrate into which they like to burrow in search of scraps of food. The water should not be too acid and from time to time a proportion should be renewed.

In the wild the species of *Corydoras* live in slow-flowing rivers, usually in shoals in fairly shallow water. They are also known to move out on to land, often on sand-banks. Here they have the advantage of being able to utilize atmospheric air for breathing. Air taken in at the mouth passes along the intestine to the hind gut where it is absorbed into the bloodstream.

Spawning is preceded by an elaborate courtship involving two or three males and one female. The males start by touching the female continuously with their snouts. This stimulates the female to swim around and to start cleaning leaves and rocks. One of the males then seizes the female's barbels with his pectoral fins, holds her against his body and sheds sperm. The female then lays 3–5 eggs into a hollow formed by pressing together her two ventral fins. She swims away through the sperm-laden water and attaches the newly fertilized eggs to the previously cleaned places.

The spawning process may be repeated several times, sometimes over a period of days. During this time most aquarists make a practice of feeding the fishes on whiteworms. After spawning the parents should be removed from the tank. The eggs hatch in 5–8 days (at 20–23°C), becoming considerably darker during their development. Some authorities recommend that the newly hatched fry should be transferred to an all-glass tank without any substrate, others prefer to leave them in the breeding tank and to change a proportion of the water.

The fry are usually not very difficult to rear. Feed them at first on very tiny live food such as brine shrimp nauplii and later on water fleas, *Tubifex* and whiteworms. If fed properly they can grow very rapidly. While young the front part of the body is green, the rear part red.

Bronze corydoras

Corydoras aeneus

Two pairs of barbels on the upper jaw. When laid back they reach the gill slits

Each flank has 21–23 upper and 19–21 lower bony plates

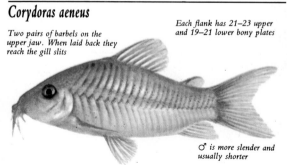

♂ is more slender and usually shorter

This is one of the best known members of the genus *Corydoras*. There is also an albino form of this species. Trinidad, Venezuela to R. de la Plata. *Length:* to 7 cm; *Diet:* cr, in, wm, vg, dr; *Water:* nc, 18–26°C; *Tank:* 40 cm

Leopard corydoras

Corydoras julii

The barbels are quite short, not reaching the lower part of the gill cover when laid back

♂ *is slimmer and usually shorter*

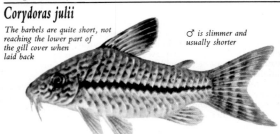

A very active species which spends most of its time moving about over the substrate picking up scraps. Has not been bred very often. Small tributaries of the lower Amazon. *Length:* to 6 cm; *Diet:* cr, in, wm, vg, dr; *Water:* nc, 18–26°C; *Tank:* 40 cm

Black-spotted corydoras

Corydoras melanistius

The male is more slender and usually shorter than the female. The barbels are quite short. R. Essequibo (Guyana). *Length:* to 6 cm; *Diet:* cr, in, wm, vg, dr; *Water:* nc, 18–26°C; *Tank:* 40 cm

Myers' corydoras

Corydoras myersi

♂ *is slimmer and shorter than ♀*

This species has three pairs of barbels. Small tributaries of the upper Amazon. *Length:* to 6 cm; *Diet:* cr, in, wm, vg, dr; *Water:* nc, 18–26°C; *Tank:* 40 cm

Peppered corydoras

Corydoras paleatus

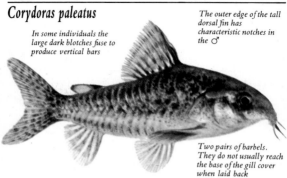

In some individuals the large dark blotches fuse to produce vertical bars

The outer edge of the tall dorsal fin has characteristic notches in the ♂

Two pairs of barbels. They do not usually reach the base of the gill cover when laid back

This is one of the most accommodating of the Corydoras catfishes and perhaps the easiest to breed. It was first bred in Paris in 1878 and has even been known to spawn successfully in a community tank. A very pale variety has been produced. South-eastern Brazil and La Plata basin. *Length:* to 7 cm; *Diet:* cr, in, wm, vg, dr; *Water:* nc, 18–26°C; *Tank:* 40 cm

Reticulated corydoras

Corydoras reticulatus

There are two pairs of fairly short barbels. The male is shorter and more brightly coloured than the female and its reticulated pattern (which is only fully developed when sexually mature) is more pronounced. Young individuals vary in colour from grey to pale red. This species is often seen resting on rocks. Monte Alegre area (Amazon basin). *Length:* to 7 cm; *Diet:* cr, in, wm, vg, dr; *Water:* nc, 18–26°C; *Tank:* 40 cm

Family Loricariidae

Found only in northern and central South America, these catfishes live on the bottom. They have 3–4 rows of bony plates along each flank. The mouth (in the form of a sucker) is positioned on the underside of the head.

Whiptail

Loricaria filamentosa

♂ has fine bristly tufts on the head

The mouth has broad lips adapted for sucking algae

Spawning takes place in a cave and the male guards the eggs which hatch in 8–10 days. The fry grow rapidly. Feed on tiny live food at first. R. Magdalena (Columbia). *Length:* to 25 cm; *Diet:* wm, vg, dr; *Water:* s-mh, 21–26°C; *Tank:* 60 cm

Golden otocinclus

Otocinclus affinis

Courtship is similar to that of the *Corydoras* species. The eggs hatch in 48 hours and the fry are free-swimming two or three days later. The tank must have plenty of algae for browsing. Rio de Janeiro area (Brazil). *Length:* to 4 cm; *Diet:* wm, vg, dr; *Water:* s-mh, 18–25°C; *Tank:* 30 cm

Otocinclus flexilis

Browses on the algae which grow in the aquarium

♀ is stouter, but there are no other external sex differences

This species is mainly active at night. It is very similar to *O. affinis* from which it differs in having rows of spots on the dorsal and anal fins. R. de la Plata. *Length:* to 6 cm; *Diet:* wm, vg, dr; *Water:* s-mh, 18–25°C; *Tank:* 30 cm

Suckermouth catfish

Plecostomus punctatus

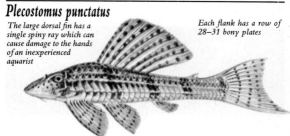

The large dorsal fin has a single spiny ray which can cause damage to the hands of an inexperienced aquarist

Each flank has a row of 28–31 bony plates

The mouth is ventral, with one pair of barbels

This catfish hides away during the day in the wild and is mainly active in twilight and at night. It is a keen remover of algae from the tank. Does not grow to full size in captivity. Southern and south-eastern Brazil. *Length:* to 30 cm; *Diet:* wm, vg, dr; *Water:* mh, sal, 18–26°C; *Tank:* 60 cm

Family Cyprinodontidae

Egg-laying toothcarps or killifishes. Relatively small fishes from North and South America, southern Europe, Africa and southern Asia. Unlike the true carps (Cyprinidae) they have teeth on the jaws and there are no barbels or adipose fin. They can be separated into two groups on the basis of their reproductive habits: in the 'non-annual' species each fish lives for one or more years (as in the Cyprinidae); the 'annual' toothcarps live in tropical waters which dry up every year. The adults die when this happens, leaving their eggs in the mud. When the rains return the eggs hatch and the young grow up, spawn and die within a single season. In the aquarium, after spawning, you should drain the eggs and substrate, allow it to dry out partially, then store in the dark for a few weeks, or longer, depending on the species.

Spanish toothcarp

Aphanius iberus

The tank should have plenty of vegetation

♂

♂ has dark dorsal and anal fins and pale blue transverse bands

♀ has colourless fins and rows of brown spots

The male swims round the female during the very active courtship. The eggs are laid on fine-leaved plants and will not be eaten if the parents are well fed. They hatch in about 7 days. Coastal areas of the western Mediterranean. *Length:* to 5 cm; *Diet:* cr, in, wm, dr; *Water:* h, sal, 10–28°C; *Tank:* 50 cm

Green panchax

Aplocheilus blocki

Spawning takes place among fine-leaved plants or on the roots of floating plants; mops of nylon wool can also be used. The eggs hatch in 12–14 days and the fry soon take brine shrimp nauplii. Sort the brood according to size at intervals to prevent cannibalism. Southern India, Sri Lanka. *Length:* to 5 cm; *Diet:* cr, in, wm, dr; *Water:* s, pt, 23–28°C; *Tank:* 30 cm

Ceylon killifish

Aplocheilus dayi

The ♀s and the young ♂'s have dark transverse bars on the rear part of the body

♂ is larger

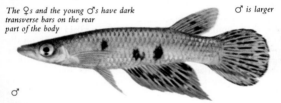

♂

Spawning continues over a period of several days. The female lays 6–10 eggs a day on the leaves and roots of plants. The eggs hatch in about 12 days and the fry can be fed on brine shrimp nauplii. Southern India, Sri Lanka. *Length:* to 9 cm; *Diet:* cr, in wm, fh, dr; *Water:* s, 20–25°C; *Tank:* 30 cm

Blue panchax

Aplocheilus panchax

Several brightly coloured selected varieties have been produced

♂ is darker and usually greyish-yellow

♂

♀ has more rounded fins

A predatory, surface-living fish, very variable in coloration over the wide range of distribution. It is easy to breed. The male drives the female very vigorously and spawning goes on for several days with the female laying 140–300 eggs in daily batches. Feed the fry on brine shrimp nauplii. They grow very rapidly and may be sexually mature in 6–8 months. North-eastern India, Burma, Thailand, Malay Archipelago. *Length:* to 8 cm; *Diet:* cr, in, wm, fh, dr; *Water:* s, 20–25°C; *Tank:* 30 cm

Java medaka

Oryzias javanicus

Lives in the upper water

♂ *has larger dorsal and anal fins*

Spawning should take place in soft water as the fry do not thrive in hard water. The female produces groups of eggs which hang from her genital opening at first but are soon rubbed off on the plants. They hatch in about 15 days. This species is often classified in a separate family, the Oryziatidae. Malay Peninsula, Java. *Length:* to 4 cm; *Diet:* cr, in, wm, dr; *Water:* nc, 24–26°C; *Tank:* 40 cm

Lyretail

Aphyosemion australe

♂ *is more colourful, with long dorsal and anal fins and a lyre-shaped tail*

♀ *is pale brown with small red spots*

♂

One of the better known African 'non-annual' toothcarps, this species is best kept in very soft water (2–4°DH) as a single pair. Spawning goes on for several days. The eggs are laid among fine-leaved plants and hatch in about two weeks. There is an orange form of this species usually known as the Golden lyretail. Cameroon, Gabon, Zaïre. *Length:* to 6 cm; *Diet:* cr, in, wm, dr; *Water:* s, ac, pt, 23–28°C; *Tank:* 30 cm

Plumed lyretail

Aphyosemion filamentosum

♂ is larger and more colourful (the red markings more vivid) with elongated anal and caudal fin rays

The edges of the fins are not divided into filaments in the ♀

An active toothcarp living mainly in the midwater and usually spawning on or near the bottom. The eggs hatch in 20–40 days but this may be difficult. Transfer them to a separate tank with care—they have very delicate shells—and keep in complete darkness. The young grow rapidly and may be sexually mature in 4 months. Sort into batches according to size to prevent cannibalism. South-western Nigeria. *Length:* to 5 cm; *Diet:* cr, in, wm, dr; *Water:* s, ac, pt, 20–24°C; *Tank:* 30 cm

Red aphyosemion

Roloffia occidentalis

This is one of the 'annual' toothcarps (see family introduction p 81). The eggs require a resting period of several weeks. Sierra Leone. *Length:* to 9 cm; *Diet:* cr, in, wm, dr; *Water:* s, ac, pt, 20–24°C; *Tank:* 30 cm

Rocket panchax

Epiplatys annulatus

Coloration (particularly of the fins) varies geographically

An elegant, small fish that is rather difficult to breed. The very small eggs are laid among the hanging roots of floating plants. They are very sensitive to bacterial infections. In the very few cases of successful breeding the eggs hatched in about 14 days. Sierra Leone, Liberia. *Length:* to 4 cm; *Diet:* cr, in dr; *Water:* s, pt, 24–28°C; *Tank:* 30 cm

Six-barred epiplatys

Epiplatys sexfasciatus

A rather timid fish which often hides away under broad leaves

♂

♀ has rounded dorsal and anal fins

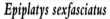

Lower half of the body has 6 transverse bars

♂ is more colourful with pointed fins

One male and two females should be put in the breeding tank. The eggs are laid singly on broad leaves close to the surface and hatch in about 14 days. The fry are not difficult to rear. This species will not always accept dried food. Liberia, Ghana, Gabon to R. Zaïre. *Length:* to 10 cm; *Diet* cr, in, wm, fh, dr; *Water:* s, ac, pt, 22–28°C; *Tank:* 40 cm

Featherfin panchax

Pterolebias longipinnis

An 'annual' species. For breeding put a sexually mature pair into a tank on their own. The tank should be all-glass with a substrate of peat. Spawning usually starts immediately and the eggs are inserted into the substrate. This may continue for two or three weeks. The eggs will only hatch after a resting period in damp peat of between one and three months (see family introduction p 81). Brazil. *Length:* to 10 cm; *Diet:* cr, in, wm, dr; *Water:* s, ac, pt, 23–26°C; *Tank:* 40 cm

Playfair's panchax

Pachypanchax playfairi

A lively, sometimes quarrelsome toothcarp which should not be kept in a tank with smaller fishes. At spawning time the scales of the male may stand out from the body, a condition reminiscent of dropsy disease but in fact quite harmless. The eggs are laid among the vegetation and hatch in 10–14 days. East Africa, Seychelles. *Length:* to 10 cm; *Diet:* cr, in, wm, fh, dr; *Water:* s, mh, 22–25°C; *Tank:* 40 cm

American flagfish

Jordanella floridae

♂ is shorter and more colourful

♀ has one conspicuous dark marking above the base of the pectoral fin and another towards the back of the dorsal fin

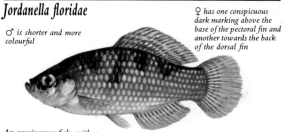

An omnivorous fish, with a preference for plant food

After a very active courtship the pair spawns in a small pit in the substrate. This is repeated for several days, with a daily production of about 20 eggs. The female must be removed at the end of spawning and the male then guards the eggs which hatch in about 6 days. After a further 14 days move the young to a separate tank with a good growth of algae on which they feed. Florida to Yucatán. *Length:* to 6 cm; *Diet:* cr, in, wm, vg, dr; *Water:* mh, alk, 19–22°C; *Tank:* 50 cm

Argentine pearlfish

Cynolebias belotti

The males are rather aggressive towards one another. This is an 'annual' species with reproductive habits similar to those of the Featherfin panchax. The female has been seen to use her anal fin to press the eggs into the substrate. In some cases both fishes may burrow into the substrate, disappearing completely, where they then spawn. La Plata basin. *Length:* to 7 cm; *Diet:* cr, in, wm, dr; *Water:* s, ac, pt, 18–30°C; *Tank:* 30 cm

Dwarf Argentine pearlfish

Cynolebias nigripinnis

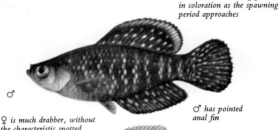

♂ *becomes increasingly vivid in coloration as the spawning period approaches*

♂

♀ *is much drabber, without the characteristic spotted pattern of the* ♂

♂ *has pointed anal fin*

♀

Should preferably be kept in a small tank

Also known as the Black-finned pearlfish. During spawning the male entices the female in the direction of the substrate (which should be peat). The fishes press close to one another, start to burrow and spawn. The eggs require a resting period of 4 months in damp peat. La Plata basin. *Length:* to 5 cm; *Diet:* cr, in, wm, dr; *Water:* s, ac, pt, 17–25°C; *Tank:* 30 cm

Lamp-eye panchax

Aplocheilichthys macrophthalmus

A shoaling species which lives at the surface of rivers. It breeds most successfully in soft, slightly acid water although it becomes more susceptible to fish tuberculosis in such conditions. Therefore it may be best kept in hard, neutral or alkaline water. West Africa. *Length:* 4 cm; *Diet:* cr, in, wm, dr; *Water:* nc, 22–26°C; *Tank:* 50 cm

Family Anablepidae

Only two species. They range from southern Mexico to northern South America and live at the surface. They are live-bearing. Each eye is divided by a horizontal bridge. The fish swims with the upper part of the eye above and the lower part below the surface, so that it sees objects in the air and in the water.

Four-eyes

Anableps anableps

This species jumps well, so the tank must have a close-fitting lid

The head is flattened, the eyes very protruding, able to see above and below the surface

The tank should have a large surface area but it can be quite shallow. The eggs develop within the body of the female who gives birth twice a year to a small number of young which are already 3–4 cm long. Northern and central South America. *Length:* to 20 cm; *Diet:* in, *Water:* sal, 23–25°C; *Tank:* 60 cm

Family Poeciliidae

Live-bearing toothcarps, originally restricted to the Americas although some species have been introduced to other warm areas to control the spread of mosquitoes. They live mainly in slow-flowing waters. The sexes show distinct differences in size and fin structure and sometimes in coloration. In the males part of the anal fin (usually the 3rd, 4th and 5th rays) develops into a gonopodium. This structure is used to insert sperm packets (spermatophores) into the genital tract of the female. The fertilized eggs develop within the female's body and the young are born live. The sperm from a single mating can fertilize several batches of eggs.

Pike top minnow

Belonesox belizanus

A predatory but shy species which lies in wait for prey

♂

The mouth is deeply cleft

♂ is much smaller and has a gonopodium

A pike-like fish, best kept as a pair, although a large female has been known to swallow her mate. The female has a gestation period of 30–50 days and may produce 20–80 live young at a time which are 16–24 mm long at birth. They start to feed on tiny crustaceans almost immediately. Southern Mexico, Guatemala, Honduras. *Length:* ♀ to 20 cm, ♂ to 12 cm; *Diet:* in, fh; *Water:* mh, alk, sal, 25–30°C; *Tank:* 80 cm

Mosquitofish

Gambusia affinis

Used for controlling mosquitoes in warm countries. It is an aggressive species and not often kept in the home aquarium. The tank should be densely planted and any algal growths should not be removed. It is not easy to breed. Feed the females on whiteworms and, if possible, mosquito larvae. The period of gestation is 5–8 weeks and the female produces 30–60 young. Protect the young from the very cannibalistic parents. Texas to Florida. *Length:* ♀ to 8 cm, ♂ to 4 cm; *Diet:* cr, in, wm, vg, dr; *Water:* nc, 18–24°C; *Tank:* 50 cm

Least killifish

Heterandria formosa

Also known as the Dwarf top minnow. An active fish which, in spite of its size, is quite aggressive. The water in the breeding tank should be 26°C and any filamentous algae be removed. The female produces live young over several days, (about two or three each day). She will chase and eat her young quite relentlessly—dense vegetation should give them some protection. South Carolina to Florida. *Length:* ♀ to 3 cm, ♂ to 2 cm; *Diet:* cr, wm, vg, dr; *Water:* mh, alk, 20–24°C; *Tank:* 30 cm

Cuban limia

Poecilia vittata

A peaceful fish, originally caught in the canal area near Havana harbour. The tank should be well lit, but care should be taken when changing the water as this species is sensitive to new water. Many aquarists recommend the addition of salt. The female produces 20–50 young after a gestation period of 3–5 weeks. They grow quite rapidly and are not attacked by the parents. Cuba. *Length:* ♀ to 9 cm, ♂ to 6 cm; *Diet:* cr, in, wm, vg, dr; *Water:* mh, alk, sal, 22–25°C; *Tank:* 50 cm

Black-bellied limia

Poecilia melanogaster

Also known as the Blue limia. This active but peaceful species does best in a tank which receives some sunshine and has plenty of open water for swimming among the plants. A healthy female will give birth every 6–8 weeks, usually to 20 or more at a time. They will disperse among the plants which helps them to escape the attentions of the female. Small streams in Jamaica and Haiti. *Length:* ♀ to 6 cm, ♂ to 4 cm; *Diet:* cr, in, wm, vg, dr; *Water:* mh, alk, sal, 22–28°C; *Tank:* 50 cm

Black molly

Poecilia hybrid

There are several varieties of Black molly, developed from the three species described here. The exact parentage of some of these forms is not known. The photograph shows two Black mollies with lyretails and three of another form. The name Molly is derived from the now superseded genus *Mollienisia*, in which these fishes were once classified. Mexico, Colombia, Venezuela, Leeward Islands. *Length:* to 10 cm; *Diet:* cr, in, wm, vg, dr; *Water:* mh, alk, sal, 23–28°C; *Tank:* 40 cm

Sailfin molly

Poecilia latipinna

The strikingly tall, sail-like dorsal fin of the male only develops fully when sexual maturity is retarded by keeping them at the lower end of the temperature range. The female gives birth to 20–80 young (10–12 mm long) after a gestation period of about two months. She should then be removed from the breeding tank. South-eastern USA, Mexico. *Length:* to 12 cm; *Diet:* cr, in, wm, vg, dr; *Water:* mh, alk, sal, 20–26°C; *Tank:* 50 cm

Mexican sailfin molly
Poecilia velifera

Reproduction is similar to that described under *P. latipinna*. The young should be fed on newly hatched brine shrimp nauplii at first and plant food is important at all stages. The photograph shows a male in courtship display with its dorsal fin fully extended. Coastal areas of Yucatán. *Length:* to 15 cm; *Diet:* cr, in, wm, vg, dr; *Water:* mh, alk, sal, 25–28°C; *Tank:* 50 cm

Pointed-mouth molly
Poecilia sphenops

Dorsal fin has
8–11 rays

♂ is shorter
and more slender

An extremely variable species, both in size and coloration. During the last 50 years several distinct varieties have been produced by specialist breeders, including completely black forms and the more colourful Liberty molly. An albino form is shown in the photograph. Mexico, Colombia, Venezuela, Leeward Islands. *Length:* to 10 cm; *Diet:* cr, in, wm, vg, dr; *Water:* mh, alk, sal, 23–28°C; *Tank:* 40 cm

Guppy

Poecilia reticulata

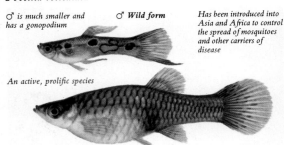

♂ is much smaller and has a gonopodium

♂ **Wild form**

Has been introduced into Asia and Africa to control the spread of mosquitoes and other carriers of disease

An active, prolific species

The wild form is easier to breed and more hardy than the domesticated forms, some of which are shown in the photograph

♀ **Wild form**

♀ is less colourful

First brought to Europe from Barbados in 1861. It was later sent from Trinidad by Robert John Lechmere Guppy to the Natural History Museum, London, hence the universally known popular name. The period of gestation depends upon the age and condition of the female but is usually 4–6 weeks and 20–100 young are produced at a time. The young grow rapidly and are fully grown at 6 months but they may become sexually mature when only two months old. The Guppy is one of the most variable of aquarium fishes, so it is not surprising that aquarists throughout the world have produced an extensive array of domesticated forms such as the Roundtail, Pintail, Lyretail, Veiltail, Flagtail, and Fantail, as well as several colour varieties. Barbados, Trinidad, South America north of R. Amazon. *Length:* ♀ to 6 cm, ♂ to 3 cm; *Diet:* cr, in, wm, vg, dr; *Water:* mh, alk, sal, 24–27°C; *Tank:* 30 cm

Swordtail

Xiphophorus helleri

♂ **Wild form**

♂ has long 'sword' tail although the body is shorter than ♀

♀ is somewhat paler

♀ **Wild form**

This species occurs in mountain streams, slow-flowing streams and swamps near coastal lagoons. It is active and requires a tank with plenty of open space for swimming and dense groups of plants to provide hiding places. A certain amount of plant food is essential. Depending on her size the female gives birth to 20–240 (rarely over 200) young after a gestation period of 4–6 weeks. The top photograph shows a female about to give birth. The bottom photograph shows a Tuxedo lyretail and a female Red lyretail. Mexico, Guatemala, Honduras. *Length:* to 12 cm; *Diet:* cr, in, wm, vg, dr; *Water:* mh, alk, 20–25°C; *Tank:* 50 cm

Platy

Xiphophorus maculatus

Lives in ponds and lakes in lowland areas with relatively low temperatures. Several local populations have arisen, varying in colour and pattern. Aquarists have produced still more variants, including true albinos and the Red platy (shown in the photograph), the Golden, Tuxedo and Wagtail platy. The female gives birth to 10–70 live young, each 7–8 mm long, after a gestation period of 4–6 weeks. Mexico, Guatemala, Belize. *Length:* ♀ to 6 cm, ♂ to 4 cm; *Diet:* cr, in, wm, vg, dr; *Water:* mh, alk, 20–25°C; *Tank:* 30 cm

Variatus platy

Xiphophorus variatus

♂ *is smaller than* ♀

This is a very active, hardy species in the aquarium

The dorsal fin has 11–13 rays

♂

A very variable, mainly lowland species living in relatively cool water. There are also numerous selected forms, such as the Red and Black variatus, the Golden- and Silver-headed variatus, the Golden- and Black-finned variatus, the Hi-fin and the Marigold platy. Provide good lighting and groups of plants. The female produces 20 or more young (up to 200 if she is large) over a period of days. Mexico. *Length:* ♀ to 7 cm, ♂ to 5.5 cm; *Diet:* cr, in, wm, vg, dr; *Water:* mh, alk, 20–25°C; *Tank:* 30 cm

Family Exocoetidae

The family includes the flying fishes (not kept in the aquarium) as well as the half-beaks. Most live in warm seas or in brackish water, a few in fresh water. The half-beaks are so named from the characteristic long lower jaw and short upper jaw.

Half-beak

Dermogenys pusillus

♂ *is shorter*

In the wild this surface-living fish feeds mainly on insects

The lower jaw is fixed but the shorter upper jaw moves with the skull

Place a pregnant female in a tank with shallow water (about 6 cm) and clumps of plants. After 4–8 weeks' gestation she produces 10–20 young (about 1 cm long). Feed initially on powdered food, after two weeks on brine shrimp nauplii. The lower jaw does not start to lengthen until about 5 weeks. Thailand, Malaya, Indonesia. *Length:* to 7 cm; *Diet:* cr, in, wm, dr; *Water:* mh, alk, sal, 22–26°C; *Tank:* 30 cm

Family Centrarchidae

Sunfishes, restricted to North America. This is a family of small to medium-sized fishes, some of which have been introduced into Europe. In some species the breeding pair spawns in shallow pits in the bottom and the male guards the brood.

Everglades pygmy sunfish

Elassoma evergladei

A very hardy fish that can be kept at 8–12°C in winter. It can sometimes be bred successfully in outdoor ponds. The eggs are laid on plants and hatch in two or three days. After using the contents of the yolk sac the fry will feed on brine shrimp nauplii. South-eastern USA. *Length:* to 3.5 cm; *Diet:* cr, vg, dr; *Water:* mh-h, alk, 15–25°C; *Tank:* 30 cm

Pumpkinseed

Lepomis gibbosus

♂ *is more slender*

♀ *is less brightly coloured*

This species needs a tank with plenty of open water for swimming, and many clumps of plants

A cold-water species successfully introduced into many parts of Europe as a pond fish

One of the most popular members of the family for the aquarium. The breeding tank should have a fine substrate, for the male uses his fins to fan a deep pit in which several hundred eggs are laid. The female should then be removed. The male will guard the nest and fan the eggs (to prevent the surrounding water from becoming stagnant) until they hatch after 4–6 days. He may continue to guard the fry. Great Lakes to Texas and Florida. *Length:* to 20 cm; *Diet:* cr, in, wm, dr; *Water:* nc, 8–22°C; *Tank:* 80 cm

Black-banded sunfish

Enneacanthus chaetodon

The male digs quite a shallow depression in the substrate and entices a female to spawn, which may produce several hundred eggs. She should then be removed. The male guards and fans the eggs and will also guard the fry but should be removed as they start to move away from the nest. Aquarists have conflicting opinions about suitable water composition for this cold-water fish. New Jersey to Maryland. *Length:* to 10 cm; *Diet:* cr, in, wm; *Water:* nc, 8–22°C; *Tank:* 40 cm

Family Centropomidae

Glassfishes. Distributed from East Africa to the Pacific, mainly in the sea and brackish waters, a few in fresh water. The body is usually thin and translucent with the backbone and internal organs clearly visible. The swimbladder is pointed at the rear in the male, rounded in the female.

Indian glassfish

Chanda ranga

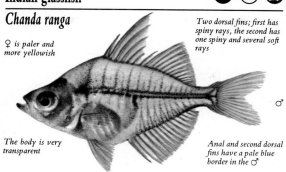

♀ is paler and more yellowish

Two dorsal fins; first has spiny rays, the second has one spiny and several soft rays

The body is very transparent

Anal and second dorsal fins have a pale blue border in the ♂

♂

Spawning is often stimulated by morning sunshine. The eggs are laid in batches of 4–6 and hatch in about 24 hours. For 3–4 days the fry hang from the plants; they should then be fed on tiny nauplii. Not easy to rear. They remain in a shoal and do not hunt for food, so aeration should be fixed to drive the food past the fry. India, Burma, Thailand. *Length:* to 6 cm; *Diet:* cr, wm, dr; *Water:* h, alk, sal, 18–25°C; *Tank:* 40 cm

Family Toxotidae

The archerfishes: one genus and 5 species distributed from India and south-east Asia to Australia and the western Pacific.

Archerfish

Toxotes jaculator

Large individuals can shoot down insects sitting on overhanging leaves at a distance of up to 150 cm

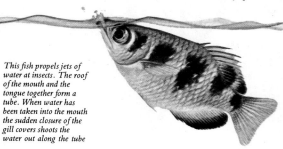

This fish propels jets of water at insects. The roof of the mouth and the tongue together form a tube. When water has been taken into the mouth the sudden closure of the gill covers shoots the water out along the tube

Lives in brackish waters and estuaries. India, Sri Lanka, south-east Asia, north-east Australia to Melanesia. *Length:* to 24 cm; *Diet:* in, wm; *Water:* mh, sal, 25–28°C; *Tank:* 80 cm

Family Monodactylidae

Fingerfishes: live in shoals in brackish and sea waters on African coasts, southern Asia, tropical Australia, and the western Pacific.

Fingerfish

Monodactylus argenteus

There are no external sex differences

The dorsal fin tip is orange in young individuals

Keep this species in brackish water. It will only thrive in fresh water when young. It is a peaceful fish which does well with other species requiring the same water conditions

Lives in a shoal and likes plenty of space for swimming

Also known as the Mono or Singapore angel. Spawning has been recorded in the aquarium, but the eggs did not hatch. Coastal areas of east Africa to Malaya and Polynesia. *Length:* to 23 cm; *Diet:* cr, in, wm, vg, dr; *Water:* mh, sal, 24–28°C; *Tank:* 80 cm

Striped fingerfish

Monodactylus sebae

There are no external sex differences

A rarely imported fish, mostly seen in public aquaria

The ventral fins are very tiny

Lives in brackish and sea water and at times in fresh water

This species can breed when it reaches a length of 10 cm

The dark transverse markings tend to become less distinct as the fish ages

Spawning is very active. The eggs (sometimes over 20,000) hatch in 20–24 hours. Senegal to Zaïre. *Length:* 20 cm; *Diet:* cr, in, wm, vg, dr; *Water:* h, alk, sal, 24–28°C; *Tank:* 80 cm

100

Family Scatophagidae

The argusfishes live along the coasts of southern and south-east Asia and northern Australia. They are omnivorous and often frequent the sewage outlets of coastal towns. The young move into brackish and fresh waters.

Argusfish

Scatophagus argus

Feeds largely on decomposing organic material in the wild, hence the generic name *Scatophagus* (dung-eater). Kept in brackish water it will feed well and grow rapidly. South-east Asia, northern Australia to the Pacific. *Length:* to 30 cm; *Diet:* cr, in, wm, vg, dr; *Water:* mh, sal, 20–28°C; *Tank:* 80 cm

Family Nandidae

Species found in northern South America, western Africa and southern Asia. This distribution points to a former close connection between South America and Africa. They are greedy predators.

Badis

Badis badis

♂ is slimmer and more colourful

Belly outline is convex in the ♀, slightly concave in ♂

A relatively peaceful member of this predatory family

The female spawns in a small cave. The eggs hatch in about three days and the male guards the fry until they have consumed the yolk sac contents. Then remove the parents. Feed the young on tiny live food. India. *Length:* to 8 cm; *Diet:* cr, in, wm, dr; *Water:* nc, 25–27°C; *Tank:* 30 cm

South American leaf-fish

Monocirrhus polyacanthus

The mouth is deeply cleft. It is rapidly protruded to snap up prey

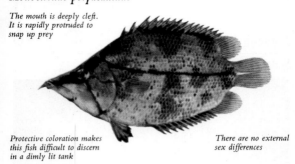

Protective coloration makes this fish difficult to discern in a dimly lit tank

There are no external sex differences

This species usually lies in wait for its prey with its head down and approaches by the imperceptible beats of the transparent pectoral fins. The eggs are attached to the underside of leaves by short filaments. They hatch in about 60 hours. Guyana, R. Negro, R. Amazon. *Length:* to 8 cm; *Diet:* fh; *Water:* s, ac, 23–28°C; *Tank:* 30 cm

Schomburgk's leaf-fish

Polycentrus schomburgki

An active predator capable of eating small earthworms and small fishes. The breeding tank should have a single pair which will spawn in a small cave. The male guards and fans the eggs which hatch in about 60 hours. The fry hang by filaments from leaves for some days and then take any small live food that passes in front of them (preferably brine shrimp nauplii). Trinidad, Venezuela, Guyana. *Length:* to 9 cm; *Diet:* in, wm, fh; *Water:* s, ac, 22–25°C; *Tank:* 30 cm

Family Cichlidae

The cichlids: a family with most of its species in America and Africa, a few in southern Asia. Unlike the true perches they have only a single nasal opening on each side of the head. Their unusual methods of reproduction make them very popular with aquarists interested in fish behaviour.

Cichlids have two main systems of reproduction, namely 'open' and 'shelter' breeding. Open breeders lay relatively few eggs in an exposed position on a rock or a large leaf. The parent fishes are similar in form and coloration, and both will guard the territory, the eggs and the young. The sexes are clearly distinguished in shelter breeders, the males being larger and brighter. Some lay their eggs in small caves where they are guarded by the female (cave breeders). In others (known as mouthbrooders), the male makes a spawning pit in his territory. After a brief courtship he leads the female to the pit where she lays some eggs which he then fertilizes. She immediately takes the eggs into her mouth where they are kept for several days, during which time she takes no food. After hatching, the fry may use the female's mouth as a refuge for a further period. In some mouthbrooders the eggs are taken into the female's mouth before fertilization. In these species the male's anal fin has a number of bright spots, resembling eggs and known as 'egg dummies'. The female snaps at these spots, presumably thinking they are eggs, and, in so doing, she sucks sperm shed by the male into her mouth, where the eggs are fertilized.

Blue acara

Aequidens pulcher

Also known as *A. latifrons*. It will spawn readily, in some cases several times a year. Provide a substrate of fine sand and a few rooted plants—the fishes do not dig very much. The eggs are laid out in the open, often on rocks, and they hatch in 2–5 days. The parents tend the eggs and remove with their mouth the white, unfertilized ones. Panama, Colombia, Trinidad, Venezuela.
Length: to 15 cm; *Diet:* cr, in, wm; *Water:* nc, 22–26°C; *Tank:* 80 cm

Keyhole cichlid

Aequidens maronii

A peaceful species which does not damage the plants, except occasionally at spawning time. The eggs are laid in the open and hatch after a few days. The parents may eat the first batch of eggs after a few days but they will then spawn again and tend the brood properly. Guyana. *Length:* to 10 cm; *Diet:* cr, in, wm; *Water:* nc, 22–25°C; *Tank:* 70 cm

Port acara

Aequidens portalegrensis

This species actively digs up the substrate, particularly during the spawning period

♂ is more greenish, ♀ is reddish with brown fins

Also known as the Black acara

This hardy species can be kept at 17–20°C in winter. It will dig up the substrate, so the tank should not contain rooted plants but rocks and floating plants are suitable. The eggs and newly hatched young are tended assiduously by both parents. Usually very prolific. The related Flag cichlid *A. curviceps* (which reaches up to 7 cm in length) is a more peaceful species. Southern Brazil, Bolivia. *Length:* to 20 cm; *Diet:* cr, in, wm, dr; *Water:* nc, 18–23°C; *Tank:* 70 cm

Agassiz's dwarf cichlid

Apistogramma agassizi

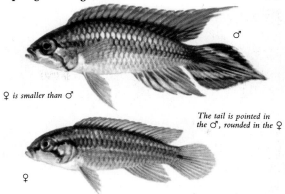

♂

♀ *is smaller than* ♂

The tail is pointed in the ♂, *rounded in the* ♀

♀

The male establishes a territory containing several smaller female territories. The male courts each female when she is ready to spawn and cleans each spawning site (a small cave). The female tends the eggs which hatch in 2–4 days. The fry are shepherded into a small pit by the female and they are free-swimming a few days later, keeping in a shoal led by the female: Amazon basin. *Length:* to 6 cm; *Diet:* cr, in, wm, dr; *Water:* s, ac, pt, 19–25°C; *Tank:* 60 cm

Yellow dwarf cichlid

Apistogramma reitzigi

Spawning and rearing is similar to Agassiz's dwarf cichlid. The female usually lays 40–60 large red eggs at a time. Her maternal instinct is very strong: if the eggs do not develop she will round up some water-fleas and protect them as though they were her own brood. Middle Paraguay. *Length:* to 6 cm; *Diet:* cr, in, wm, dr; *Water:* s, ac, pt, 23–25°C; *Tank:* 50 cm

Oscar

Astronotus ocellatus

Fond of eating snails

Also known as the Velvet cichlid

There are no reliable sex differences

Quite a peaceful cichlid in spite of its size, but a keen digger, so the tank should contain no rooted plants. The eggs are laid out in the open, usually on rocks, and there may be 600–700 at a spawning. The brood is protected by both parents. There are several varieties including a Red oscar (with large red patches on the flanks) and a Gold oscar. R. Negro, R. Amazon, R. Paraguay. *Length:* to 30 cm; *Diet:* cr, in, wm, mt, dr; *Water:* nc, 22–27°C; *Tank:* 80 cm

Jack Dempsey

Cichlasoma octofasciatum

Also known as *C. biocellatum*. A pugnacious cichlid, particularly at spawning time, hence the popular name. The tank should have no rooted plants as this is a keen digger. Spawning takes place in a large pit, where the female lays up to 600 eggs. The parent fishes guard the eggs and fry very assiduously. A proportion of the tank water should be replaced at frequent intervals. R. Negro, Middle Amazon. *Length:* to 18 cm; *Diet:* cr, in, wm, fh, mt, dr; *Water:* nc, 20–25°C; *Tank:* 80 cm

This aggressive cichlid is a fairly recent introduction to the aquarium. The best way to find breeding pairs is to rear 8–10 young in a spacious tank and let each find its own partner. The female has been known to lay up to 1,000 eggs. In the young stages the flanks are a dull brownish colour, the red only appearing when the fishes are about two years old. Exact distribution unknown. *Length:* to 25 cm; *Diet:* cr, in, wm, fh, mt, dr; *Water:* nc, 20–25°C; *Tank:* 100 cm

Festivum

Cichlasoma festivum

Also known as the Barred cichlid

Lives alongside Angelfishes in the wild

At spawning time the genital papilla is pointed in the ♂, rounded in the ♀

Unlike many of its relatives this is a peaceful and rather shy cichlid. Keep in a tank with clumps of plants and a few tree roots to provide hiding places. The eggs are laid on plants and hatch in two or three days (at 26°C). The fry hang from leaves for a further couple of days and are then free-swimming. Western Guyana, R. Amazon. *Length:* to 15 cm; *Diet:* cr, in, wm, vg, dr; *Water:* nc, 20–26°C; *Tank:* 60 cm

Firemouth cichlid

Cichlasoma meeki

A peaceful cichlid, except at spawning time

Only a half-hearted digger so the tank can have a few plants with tough leaves. It can start to breed when about 8 cm long and spawns as the other species of *Cichlasoma*. Has also been found in underground waters. Yucatán, Guatemala. *Length:* to 15 cm; *Diet:* cr, in, wm, dr; *Water:* nc, 20–25°C; *Tank:* 60 cm

Zebra cichlid

Cichlasoma nigrofasciatum

Also known as the convict cichlid

♂ has more elongated fins and is brighter

An aggressive cichlid. Requires a plentiful vegetable diet. Spawns as the other species of *Cichlasoma*. L. Atitlán and L. Amatitlán (Guatemala). *Length:* to 10 cm; *Diet:* cr, in, wm, fh, mt, vg, dr; *Water:* nc, 20–26°C; *Tank:* 80 cm

Earth-eater

Geophagus jurupari

♂ is more slender and the fins are slightly more prolonged

'Munches' the substrate in search of food

The breeding tank should have a substrate of fine sand. The eggs are laid on a rock. These are mouthbrooders (see family introduction p 103). Guyana, north-eastern Brazil. *Length:* to 25 cm; *Diet:* cr, in, wm; *Water:* nc, 22–28°C; *Tank:* 60 cm

Rio Grande perch

Herichthys cyanoguttatus

Also known as the Texas cichlid; the only cichlid to occur naturally in the USA. A fairly aggressive species and an enthusiastic uprooter of plants. A proportion of the water should be renewed at intervals. Spawning takes place on a previously cleaned stone and the female lays about 500 eggs which hatch in 5–7 days. The parents are sometimes lax in protecting the young. Texas, northern Mexico. *Length:* to 25 cm; *Diet:* cr, in, wm, mt, vg; *Water:* nc, 15–25°C; *Tank:* 80 cm

Pike cichlid

Crenicichla lepidota

The mouth is deeply cleft

A highly predatory cichlid, dangerous to anything not approaching its own size: prey is seized head first and swallowed. Not such a ready spawner as the species of *Cichlasoma*. The tiny white eggs are laid in a shallow pit in the substrate and protected mainly by the male which should be fed copiously during this period on large insects or small fishes. Brazil, Paraguay, Uruguay, northern Argentina. *Length:* to 20 cm; *Diet:* in, wm, fh; *Water:* nc, 20–26°C; *Tank:* 80 cm

Golden-eyed dwarf cichlid

Nannacara anomala

♀ is smaller and less colourful

♀

Does not usually dig up the substrate to any extent

Fins do not have coloured borders in the ♀

♂

A peaceful species. Keep in a tank with plenty of plants and some rocks and tree roots for hiding places. Remove the male after spawning. The eggs are laid in a small cavity and guarded by the female. They hatch in two or three days and the female moves the fry to a shallow pit in the substrate. After 4–5 days feed them on very fine food. Western Guyana. *Length:* ♀ to 8 cm, ♂ to 6 cm; *Diet:* cr, in, wm; *Water:* s, ac, pt, 22–28°C; *Tank:* 50 cm

Jewel cichlid

Hemichromis bimaculatus

An active, sometimes aggressive fish. The eggs are laid on rocks or in a cave and hatch in 3–5 days. The parent fishes move the fry to a shallow pit. Old individuals can become intolerant and should be kept as a pair in a tank on their own. R. Niger, R. Zaïre, R. Nile. *Length:* to 15 cm; *Diet:* cr, in, wm, mt; *Water:* nc, 24–26°C; *Tank:* 70 cm

Pterophyllum scalare

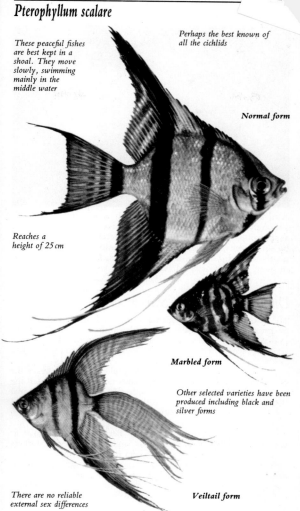

These peaceful fishes are best kept in a shoal. They move slowly, swimming mainly in the middle water

Perhaps the best known of all the cichlids

Normal form

Reaches a height of 25 cm

Marbled form

Other selected varieties have been produced including black and silver forms

There are no reliable external sex differences

Veiltail form

Keep in a tall tank with plenty of plants and some rocks. A proportion of the water should be changed regularly. Many aquarists rear a number of young fishes and allow them to find their own mates. Both partners clean the spawning site (often a leaf) and also fan the eggs which hatch in 25–35 hours. The parents gently chew the egg membranes to release the fry which at first hang by filaments from the leaves. They are free-swimming after 4–5 days and should then be fed on rotifers and brine shrimp nauplii. Amazon basin. *Length:* to 15 cm; *Diet:* cr, in, wm, vg, dr; *Water:* nc, 22–30°C; *Tank:* 60 cm

Uaru amphiacanthoides

Also known as the Triangle cichlid. It is peaceful in general, although the males may become aggressive towards one another at spawning time. Spawns in a small cave. The eggs are guarded by the parents, or they can be moved into a separate tank and gently aerated. Guyana, R. Amazon. *Length:* to 25 cm; *Diet:* cr, in, wm; *Water:* s, ac, pt, 27–30°C; *Tank:* 80 cm

Discus fishes (genus *Symphysodon*)

The discus fishes are perhaps the most handsome of all tropical freshwater aquarium fishes and are also among the most difficult to maintain in good condition. They were first introduced to the aquarium world in the early 1920s but were not bred until the late 1950s.

They require a large, tall tank with plenty of open space for swimming, a dark substrate and plants tall enough to reach the surface with floating leaves. Provide a few rocks for additional shelter. The water should be soft and slightly acid (2–4°DH, pH c. 6.5) with continuous filtration. Renew a proportion at frequent intervals.

Some aquarists provide a varied diet of live food such as whiteworms, *Tubifex*, water-fleas and insect larvae. Others prefer to use spinach or chopped beef heart.

Breeding may take place any time after the fishes are two or three years old. After a peaceful courtship the pair will spawn and the eggs are laid on rocks or leaves which have been cleaned beforehand. They hatch in about 48 hours. The parent fishes gently chew the egg membranes to release the fry, which then move to leaves where they hang by short filaments for a further two or three days. The next stage is most unusual: the fry attach themselves to the flanks of the parents, where they will feed on a secretion produced by the gland cells in the parents' skin. This process is comparable to the suckling of a new-born mammal. After a few more days the young start to move away from the parents and they should then be fed on rotifers and brine shrimp larvae. They will acquire the adult shape at about 3–4 months.

There is still argument about the scientific naming of the discus fishes: some authorities recognize two species, one with three subspecies.

Symphysodon aequifasciata haraldi

The fry feed on the secretion from the flanks of one or both parents. They begin to take other food when they reach about 1 cm and, if well fed, will grow rapidly.

The photographs show the wide colour variation in this species. This variation is also seen in the Green discus *S. aequifasciata aequifasciata*. They are both peaceful, shoaling cichlids. Manacapuru area (R. Amazon). *Length:* to 12 cm; *Diet:* cr, in, wm, vg; *Water:* s, ac, pt, 24–30°C; *Tank:* 100 cm

Brown discus

Symphysodon aequifasciata axelrodi

There are no reliable external sex differences

A peaceful cichlid. Belém area (R. Amazon). *Length:* to 14 cm; *Diet:* cr, in, wm, vg; *Water:* s, ac, pt, 24–30°C; *Tank:* 100 cm

Discus

Symphysodon discus

A peaceful cichlid. Lives in shoals in the middle and lower water. There are no reliable external sex differences. R. Negro, middle Amazon. *Length:* to 20 cm; *Diet:* cr, in, wm, vg; *Water:* s, ac, pt, 24–30°C; *Tank:* 100 cm

Green chromide

Etroplus suratensis

This peaceful species is best kept in a shoal

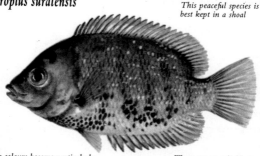

The colours become particularly brilliant at spawning time, but are otherwise fairly dull

There are no reliable sex differences, except the shape of the genital papilla

Best kept in brackish water which should be made up by dissolving two or three teaspoons of sea salt in 10 litres of tank water. The fish becomes sexually mature when it reaches a length of 12–15 cm. The eggs are laid on rocks. Both parents guard the eggs and the fry. The young are subject to fungal infections if kept in fresh water. Sri Lanka. *Length:* to 40 cm; *Diet:* in, wm, mt; *Water:* h, sal, 23–28°C; *Tank:* 80 cm

Orange chromide

Etroplus maculatus

A peaceful cichlid, which does not attack the plants

More suitable for most home aquaria than the Green chromide in view of its modest size

There are no reliable sex differences, except in the shape of the genital papilla

Keep in brackish water (as above). The black eggs are usually laid on flat stones, to which they are attached by short stalks. They are guarded by both parents and in 4–6 days hatch into fry which are similarly tended. The young are quite easy to rear. It is important to avoid any form of disturbance in the vicinity as the parents are usually rather nervous. Coastal areas of India and Sri Lanka. *Length:* to 8 cm; *Diet:* cr, in, wm, fh, vg, dr; *Water:* h, sal, 20–26°C; *Tank:* 50 cm

Egyptian mouthbrooder

Pseudocrenilabrus multicolor

Very suitable for
the home aquarium

♀

Fry

♂ has a bright red border
to the anal fin

The male digs a shallow pit to which he leads the female. They spawn above the pit and produce 30–70 eggs which the female immediately takes into her mouth where they remain for 10–12 days. During this period she does not feed. After hatching, the fry remain in or near her mouth for a further 4–5 days. Egypt to Tanzania. *Length:* to 8 cm; *Diet:* cr, in, wm, mt, dr; *Water:* nc, 20–25°C; *Tank:* 40 cm

Dimidiatus

Nanochromis dimidiatus

It is best to keep only one male with 3–4 females in a species tank. The males show very marked territorial behaviour. The female lays 70–100 yellowish eggs which hatch in 3–4 days and the young are free-swimming after a further three days. The brood is protected by the female. Zaïre. *Length:* to 7 cm; *Diet:* cr, in, wm, dr; *Water:* s, ac, pt, 22–27°C; *Tank:* 60 cm

Kribensis

Pelvicachromis pulcher

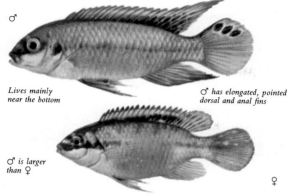

♂

Lives mainly near the bottom

♂ has elongated, pointed dorsal and anal fins

♂ is larger than ♀

♀

Formerly known as *Pelmatochromis kribensis*. It comes from coastal areas and needs brackish water (made up with 2 teaspoons of sea salt to 10 litres of water). The eggs are laid in a small cave and guarded by both parents. They hatch in two or three days and the young are free-swimming about 4 days later. Nigeria. *Length:* to 8 cm; *Diet:* cr, in, wm, dr; *Water:* nc, sal, 24–27°C; *Tank:* 60 cm

Fuelleborn's cichlid

Labeotropheus fuelleborni

One of a large group of brightly coloured cichlids from Lake Malawi which have been introduced to the aquarium world relatively recently. This species occurs in different colour forms, showing polymorphism. The males are all-blue; some of the females are blue with darker transverse bands, but others are orange with black markings. The eggs are incubated in the mouth of the female. Lake Malawi. *Length:* to 14 cm; *Diet:* cr, in, wm, vg, dr; *Water:* mh, 22–25°C; *Tank:* 80 cm

Trewavas's cichlid

Labeotropheus trewavasae

♂

♂ is always blue

♀ is either blue or marbled orange, brown and black

♀

The teeth are adapted for scraping algae off rocks

Another example of polymorphism, with colour forms similar to those in Fuelleborn's cichlid. The female lays a relatively small number of eggs, sometimes only 10–15, and these are rich in yolk. They are incubated in her mouth for 22–30 days. Lake Malawi. *Length:* to 12 cm; *Diet:* cr, in, wm, vg, dr; *Water:* mh, 22–25°C; *Tank:* 80 cm

Malawi golden cichlid

Pseudotropheus auratus

Caught along the rocky shores of the lake. The females are golden with three distinct longitudinal black bands. During the breeding period the males are almost black but when disturbed they may undergo an astonishing colour change, rapidly assuming the female coloration. The eggs are incubated in the mouth of the female. Lake Malawi. *Length:* to 12 cm; *Diet:* cr, in, wm, vg, dr; *Water:* mh, 22–25°C; *Tank:* 60 cm

Malawi blue cichlid

Pseudotropheus zebra

One of the larger Lake Malawi cichlids. Coloration is variable but there are usually 6 dark transverse bars on each flank. The male has prominent yellowish egg dummies on the anal fin. The eggs are incubated in the mouth of the female. Lake Malawi. *Length:* to 15 cm; *Diet:* cr, in, wm, vg, dr; *Water:* mh, 22–25°C; *Tank:* 60 cm

Golden julie

Julidochromis ornatus

♂ is shorter and more slender than ♀

Lives among rocks in the wild

The male sets up his territory, usually on a stone with a hollow beneath it. Here the breeding pair swims in circles until the female turns upside-down and lays several rows of eggs on the underside of the stone. The male also turns upside-down to shed sperm over the eggs. After hatching, the tiny fry (about 5 mm long) adhere to the stone for 5–6 days; they then break loose but remain near by. Lake Tanganyika. *Length:* to 8 cm; *Diet:* cr, in, wm, vg, dr; *Water:* h, 22–25°C; *Tank:* 50 cm

Tropheus spp.

The juveniles of the very similar *T. duboisi* and *T. moorii* live together but the adults do not and they do not interbreed. In the wild *T. duboisi* lives singly or in pairs at depths of 3–12 m; *T. moorii* lives in small shoals at depths of 0.5–1 m. *T. duboisi* is a mouthbrooder. 5–10 large eggs are incubated at a time; they hatch after about 40 days. Lake Tanganyika. *Length:* to 8 cm; *Diet:* cr, in, wm, vg, dr; *Water:* h, 22–25°C; *Tank:* 50 cm

Mozambique mouthbrooder

Sarotherodon mossambicus

The eggs are incubated in the female's mouth. The fry return to the shelter of her mouth when there is a sign of danger

At spawning time the ♂ becomes blue, the dorsal and anal fins become red (or at least develop a red border)

♂

An important food fish in eastern Africa. It is one of the most adaptable of all tropical freshwater fishes: it has even bred in sea water. Renew a proportion of the water frequently as this gross feeder produces much waste. The male digs a large spawning pit in the substrate. Originally eastern Africa, introduced into parts of Indonesia. *Length:* to 35 cm; *Diet:* cr, in, wm, mt, vg, dr; *Water:* nc, 21–26°C; *Tank:* 100 cm

Family Gobiidae

Gobies. Many species live in tidal or shallow coastal waters, a few live in fresh waters. The ventral fins unite at the base to form a suction organ, enabling the fish to attach itself to rocks.

Bumblebee fish

Brachygobius xanthozona

♂ is smaller than the ♀

This shy species needs plenty of hiding places in the tank

Lives in the middle and lower water

Not an easy fish to breed. In some cases spawning has been stimulated by adding some new water. The eggs are laid in a cavity and the male guards them. They hatch in 4–5 days. Borneo, Sumatra, Java. *Length:* to 4.5 cm; *Diet:* cr, in, wm, dr; *Water:* h, alk, sal, 23–30°C; *Tank:* 30 cm

Suborder Anabantoidei

The labyrinth fishes, found in Africa and south-east Asia. This suborder now contains 4 families (the Anabantidae, Belontiidae, Helostomatidae and Osphronemidae), which were formerly classified in the single family Anabantidae. Many species build a nest of air bubbles.

The Labyrinth organ

The popular name of these fishes refers to the organ situated in the upper part of the gill cavity. It has a much-folded mass of tissue, richly supplied with blood vessels and acts as an accessory respiratory organ. This allows the fish to breathe air at the surface

Climbing perch

Anabas testudineus

A rather aggressive fish in the aquarium

Uses pectoral fins and gill covers as props when moving overland

♂ has longer dorsal and anal fins

In the wild this species moves overland during wet weather. It survives this unfishlike behaviour by taking air into the labyrinth organ and using its tail for propulsion. The eggs are laid at random. India, south-east Asia. *Length:* to 25 cm; *Diet:* cr, in, wm, vg, dr; *Water:* nc, 25–30°C; *Tank:* 60 cm

Combtail

Belontia signata

♂ *is more colourful with more elongated fins*

♂ *protects the brood*

♂

The male normally builds a bubble-nest at the surface which he guards assiduously after spawning. However, there have been reports of this species spawning without a bubble-nest at the surface. The eggs hatch in about 24 hours and the fry can be fed on brine shrimp nauplii. Sri Lanka. *Length:* to 15 cm; *Diet:* cr, in, wm, dr; *Water:* nc, 24–29°C; *Tank:* 40 cm

Siamese fighting fish

Betta splendens

The males fight one another viciously, tearing the fins to shreds. This behaviour has led to staged contests in Thailand and elsewhere. A single male can be kept in a 10 cm tank. If kept in a community tank there must, of course, be only one male. There are several domesticated forms with blue, green, red or violet coloration. They are bubble-nest builders. The related species *B. brederi* from Java and Sumatra is a mouthbrooder. Originally south-east Asia. *Length:* to 6 cm; *Diet:* cr, in, wm, dr; *Water:* nc, 26–30°C; *Tank:* 50 cm

Honey gourami

Colisa chuna

This species can be kept in a community tank but the males will not then develop their full coloration — possibly due to the disturbance in the tank. They breed quite readily and build a small, poorly constructed bubble-nest. The throat and breast of the male are bluish-green to black during the breeding period. North-eastern India, Bangladesh. *Length:* to 4.5 cm; *Diet:* cr, in, wm, dr; *Water:* nc, 24–26°C; *Tank:* 30 cm

Banded gourami

Colisa fasciata

♀ *is less colourful*

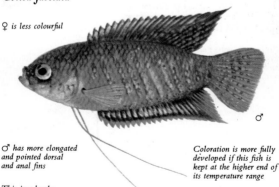

♂

♂ has more elongated and pointed dorsal and anal fins

Coloration is more fully developed if this fish is kept at the higher end of its temperature range

This is a hardy, peaceful species

The male builds a large bubble-nest which may be over 10 cm across. A single spawning yields 600–1,000 eggs. The Thick-lipped gourami *C. labiosa* is very similar—it is possible that the two species are identical. India, Burma, Thailand, Malaysia. *Length:* to 10 cm; *Diet:* cr, in, wm, dr; *Water:* nc, 20–26°C; *Tank:* 40 cm

Dwarf gourami

Colisa lalia

One of the most popular anabantoids. The tank should be well lit and preferably receive some sunshine. The light will encourage algae to grow but this should not be removed as it has been found that algae are favourable to breeding. The bubble-nest is fairly wide and usually a large amount of plant material is incorporated in it. North-east India, Bangladesh. *Length:* to 5 cm; *Diet:* cr, in, wm, dr; *Water:* nc, 20–26°C; *Tank:* 30 cm

Brown spike-tailed paradisefish

Macropodus cupanus dayi

The central points of the dorsal and anal fins are much elongated and extend over the caudal fin

In the wild this species lives in coastal districts

This is a relative of the Spike-tailed paradisefish *M. cupanus cupanus* which comes from India and Sri Lanka. It is a peaceful labyrinth fish which will tolerate relatively low temperatures, although the colours are better developed at higher temperatures. The male builds and guards a fairly small bubble-nest in which the eggs develop. The female should be removed after spawning. Malabar Coast, Burma and Vietnam. *Length:* to 7.5 cm; *Diet:* cr, in, wm, dr; *Water:* nc, 15–24°C; *Tank:* 30 cm

Paradisefish

Macropodus opercularis

Can be aggressive. Keep only with larger fishes in a community tank

♀ *is less colourful, with red bars only on the flanks*

♂ *has more elongated fins*

This species can breed when it reaches a length of about 6 cm. After spawning, the eggs float and are then collected by the male who spits them into the nest, which he guards very aggressively, so it is best to remove the female at this point. This fish is a splendid consumer of the planarians which often infest the tank. South-east Asia. *Length:* to 9 cm; *Diet:* cr, in, wm, vg, dr; *Water:* nc, 15–24°C; *Tank:* 40 cm

Gourami

Osphronemus goramy

In parts of south-east Asia this species is eaten and is said to be tasty

In the wild this peaceful fish lives in clear waters

In a sufficiently large tank this fish will grow rapidly and will soon become a burden in the home aquarium. Specimens 30–40 cm in length are not uncommon in public aquaria. They should be kept only with other large fishes. The vegetable part of the diet is essential. The male builds a bubble-nest and guards the brood. Sumatra, Borneo, Java. *Length:* to 50 cm; *Diet:* cr, in, wm, vg, dr; *Water:* nc, 18–26°C; *Tank:* 70 cm

Kissing gourami

Helostoma temmincki

The pink form illustrated is probably a variety of the less commonly seen green form

The forehead region is concave, particularly in young specimens

Prefers to feed on plant food

There are no reliable external sex differences

When browsing on algae the broad lips are protruded, as they are when two fishes touch one another, sometimes lip to lip, hence the popular name. However, this is probably a form of threat display. They become sexually mature when 3–4 years old. The pair spawns after a stormy courtship, with much splashing of water over the edge of the tank. The eggs float to the surface and adhere to plants. Thailand, Malaysia, Borneo, Sumatra, Java. *Length:* to 30 cm; *Diet:* cr, in, wm, vg, dr; *Water:* nc, 20–28°C; *Tank:* 60 cm

Chocolate gourami

Sphaerichthys osphromenoides

This fish is difficult to breed. At one time it was thought to be a live-bearer. It is now known to be a mouthbrooder, although sometimes a nest is made with plant fragments and a few bubbles. Some reports say the female carries the eggs around in her mouth for a time and then spits them into the nest. The young are slow-growing and not easy to rear. Not a fish for the beginner. Malaysia, Sumatra. *Length:* to 6 cm; *Diet:* cr, in; *Water:* s, ac, pt, 26–30°C; *Tank:* 40 cm

Pearl gourami

Trichogaster leeri

This very peaceful fish is suitable for the beginner. The male builds a relatively large bubble-nest below which the pair has an active courtship. The eggs hatch in 20–30 hours and the fry remain in the nest for a further 3–5 days, living on the contents of the yolk sacs. The male tends them, spitting any stragglers back into the nest. As soon as they finally leave the nest the male should be removed. Thailand, Malaysia, Borneo, Sumatra. *Length:* to 11 cm; *Diet:* cr, in, wm, dr; *Water:* nc, 23–30°C; *Tank:* 50 cm

Three-spot gourami

Trichogaster trichopterus

This species can breed when it reaches a length of about 6 cm. ♂ tends the brood

♂ has longer and more pointed dorsal and anal fins

The filamentous ventral fins usually reach back to the caudal fin

The male becomes very boisterous during the active courtship. Breeding habits are similar to those of the Pearl gourami. Sort out the young for size regularly to prevent cannibalism. The subspecies *T. trichopterus sumatranus* is blue and there is a form with blue and white checks, known as the Cosby. Thailand, Malaysia, Borneo, Sumatra, Java, Bali. *Length:* to 15 cm; *Diet:* cr, in, wm, dr; *Water:* nc, 20–26°C; *Tank:* 50 cm

Dwarf climbing perch

Ctenopoma nanum

One of the smaller members of its genus: a suitable African labyrinth fish for the home aquarium

♂ *is larger and slightly more colourful*

The male builds a bubble-nest and courtship takes place beneath it, the male curling around the female. There may be several spawnings, each producing about 20 eggs, with a total of several hundreds. In the Banded climbing perch *C. fasciolatum*, the nest may contain up to 1,000 eggs. Southern Cameroon, Zaïre. *Length:* to 7 cm; *Diet:* cr, in, wm, fh, dr; *Water:* s, ac, pt, 26–29°C; *Tank:* 40 cm

Suborder Atherinoidei

This suborder contains the families Melanotaeniidae (with the genus *Melanotaenia*) and Atherinidae (with the genera *Bedotia* and *Telmatherina*). Most species live in tropical shallow coastal waters, some in fresh waters.

Dwarf rainbowfish

Melanotaenia maccullochi

There are two dorsal fins

♂

♂ *is more colourful and the first dorsal fin is pointed*

A peaceful fish best kept in a small shoal. Spawning takes place in the morning sunshine, often on several mornings in succession. The eggs hang from the plants by short filaments and hatch in about 9 days (at 25°C). Feed the fry on tiny live food at first. North-eastern Australia. *Length:* to 7 cm; *Diet:* cr, in, wm, dr; *Water:* mh, 20–25°C; *Tank:* 50 cm

Red-tailed rainbowfish

Melanotaenia nigrans

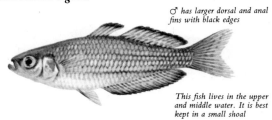

♂ *has larger dorsal and anal*
fins with black edges

This fish lives in the upper
and middle water. It is best
kept in a small shoal

Keep this species in brackish water. Breeding habits are similar to
those of *M. macullochi*. The parent fishes do not molest their
brood in either species, so they can be left in the spawning tank.
The growth rate of the fry increases after they reach a length of
about 1 cm. Southern Australia to New South Wales. *Length:* to
10 cm; *Diet:* cr, in, wm, dr; *Water:* mh-h, sal, 18–26°C; *Tank:*
60 cm

Celebes sailfish

Telmatherina ladigesi

The anal and dorsal fins of the male have elongated rays.
Spawning takes place over a period of days, usually in the
morning sunshine. The first mating produces 30–50 eggs, later
ones produce fewer. Remove the parent fishes to another tank at
the end of spawning. The eggs hatch in about 10 days and the fry
can be fed on tiny nauplii at first. Sulawesi (Celebes). *Length:* to
8 cm; *Diet:* cr, in, wm, dr; *Water:* mh, sal, 22–25°C; *Tank:* 60 cm

Madagascar rainbowfish

Bedotia geayi

The first dorsal fin is pointed in ♂, rounded in ♀

♂ has caudal and second dorsal fins edged with red

♀ is less colourful

This active fish lives in the midwater

Food is mostly taken from near the surface. Provide a supplement of vegetable matter (such as boiled lettuce). The eggs are laid among the plants, to which they adhere. They hatch in about 7 days and the fry will feed at first on rotifers, later on brine shrimp nauplii. Aerate the water vigorously to keep the food on the move. Madagascar. *Length:* to 15 cm; *Diet:* cr, in, wm, vg, dr; *Water:* mh, sal, 20–25°C; *Tank:* 60 cm

Family Gasterosteidae

Sticklebacks are cold-water fishes that live in the sea and in fresh and brackish waters. In many species the male builds a nest of plant fragments. The body is covered with bony plates and there are three or more spines at the front of the dorsal fin.

Three-spined stickleback

Gasterosteus aculeatus

At spawning time the ♂ develops an orange-red belly and the iris becomes bright green

A cold-water species

This fish is best kept in a shoal

The male builds a nest, mainly of plant matter, in the centre of his territory at the bottom of the tank. He then courts a female and entices her to enter the nest. There she lays her eggs, over which he immediately sheds sperm. He then repeats the process with other females. The eggs (which hatch in 12–15 days) and the young are guarded by the male. Northern America, Europe, northern Asia, Japan. *Length:* to 10 cm; *Diet:* cr, in, wm, fh; *Water:* nc, 4–20°C; *Tank:* 50 cm

Ten-spined stickleback

Pungitius pungitius

In the wild this cold-water species breeds from April to July. The male builds, among dense vegetation, a nest of plant fragments cemented together with a secretion from his kidneys. Courtship, spawning and brood protection take place as in the Three-spined stickleback. Northern America, Europe, northern Asia. *Length:* to 10 cm; *Diet:* cr, in, wm; *Water:* nc, 4–20°C; *Tank:* 40 cm

Family Tetraodontidae

The pufferfishes: found in warm seas, fresh and brackish waters. The powerful 'beaks' are capable of breaking mollusc shells.

Green pufferfish

Tetraodon fluviatilis

The skin is leathery and covered with small spines

Able to inflate the body if attacked

There are no external sex differences

Before spawning, the male and female circle around one another a short distance above the bottom. The female lays her translucent eggs on rocks and the male guards them, covering them with his body. They hatch in 6–9 days and the male moves the fry to small pits where he continues to guard them. South-east Asia. *Length:* to 15 cm; *Diet:* cr, in, wm, mt, vg; *Water:* nc, sal, 22–26°C; *Tank:* 50 cm

Marine fishes

Marine aquarium fishes are mostly imported
from the tropical coral reef areas. They are
usually colourful and exotic looking, making a
rewarding sight in the home aquarium, but
they are difficult to keep successfully. Many
can be kept in the aquarium only when young
as they become increasingly aggressive and
grow to an unmanageable size.

In some species (especially the angelfishes
and wrasses) the juveniles are a totally different
colour and pattern from the adults.

The marine aquarium

Tropical marine fishes are generally more difficult to keep than freshwater fishes. Many species require some time to adapt to the aquarium and should be introduced to their new habitat with care—a constant water composition must be maintained.

It is important to find compatible species. In general, it is better to buy juvenile fishes as they adapt to the aquarium more easily and tend to get on well together, although they can become quarrelsome as they approach sexual maturity. Some marine fishes are fiercely territorial. Others, such as the clownfishes, live quite happily in small groups.

Setting up the tank

The tank should preferably by 80–100 cm long; the height and width both measuring approximately half the length. The glass panes of the tank should be cemented together with silicone glue. Angle iron tanks can be used only if the metal is coated with plastic to prevent corrosion.

Substrate This should not be deeper than 3–4 cm. It should consist of coarse sand, or coral sand (broken fragments of dead coral from tropical seas) which helps to keep the water alkaline. A soft, sandy substrate is suitable for fishes which bury themselves at night, such as wrasses.

Rocks and coral skeletons can be arranged to divide the tank up into compartments so that the more territorial species are kept out of sight of each other. Non-metallic rocks such as granite may be used. Coral skeletons must be soaked for 48 hours in a solution of one part hypochlorite to 5 parts water, and then thoroughly washed in fresh water.

Do not grow ordinary seaweeds. There is, however, a small green alga, *Caulerpa*, which grows well in a marine tank.

Water

Natural sea water is a very constant medium consisting of a mixture of dissolved salts in a concentration of 35 parts per 1,000. This composition should be reproduced as closely as possible in the aquarium, and it is probably more reliable to use a ready-made mixture of salts obtainable from an aquarium dealer. Follow the instructions given on the package: dissolve the salts in tap water in a plastic container (never use metal objects in or near a marine tank) and aerate. The final product should have a pH of approximately 8.0–8.3 (see p 6). The pH of the water should be measured about once a month as it tends to fall in the closed environment of the aquarium. If it falls below 8 add a small amount of sodium carbonate to the water to bring it up to the correct alkalinity.

Depending upon the number of fishes in the tank, the waste products will soon build up to a dangerous level. The waste is broken down by bacteria to ammonia and then to nitrites and nitrates. The concentration of these chemicals can be kept at a safe level by a monthly replacement of about 30 per cent of the water with a freshly made solution of sea salts.

Temperature

For the tropical species the water should be kept at a temperature of about 26–27°C. For subtropical fishes, such as those from the Mediterranean, the water should be kept at a temperature of 16–20°C. Thermostatically controlled heaters, such as those used for freshwater tanks, should be used.

Filtration and aeration

Unlike the freshwater aquarium, the marine tank must have filtration. The motorized filter should be capable of turning over the contents of the tank at least three times an hour. Aeration also

134

helps to keep the water moving, simulating the rapid water movements experienced on a coral reef.

Lighting

The tank should be lit for 10–12 hours every day by fluorescent tubes, fitted to give about 100 watts for every 200 litres of water, thus reproducing the brilliant light conditions on a tropical reef.

Food

It may at first be difficult to get the fishes to feed in the aquarium, although the juveniles are usually more adaptable. Most marine fishes will in time feed on many of the various foods taken by freshwater fishes, including freeze-dried foods, but the more live food they get the better. This should consist mainly of worms and small crustaceans. Chopped raw fish is also suitable. In the wild some marine fishes browse on the algae growing on rocks and dead coral heads. In the aquarium such fishes will appreciate a supplement of vegetable matter such as chopped spinach.

Breeding

Very few marine fishes have bred in the aquarium. They may well be inhibited by the lack of space, which affects the behaviour patterns that lead to mating and spawning.

Disease

Like their freshwater relatives, marine fishes usually suffer from disease when they lose their resistance owing to poor feeding, incorrect temperature or other environmental disturbances. The commonest and most feared infection is caused by the microscopic organism *Oodinium ocellatum*. This appears as a fine powder covering the body. It can be treated with a copper sulphate solution, (1 g copper sulphate in 1.2 litres of water). Use 1 ml of this solution for every 2.5 litres of water. Some fishes such as the butterflyfishes do not tolerate this concentration of copper, and for them it should be reduced by 30 per cent. For this treatment the fishes do not normally need to be transferred to a separate tank. This copper treatment must not be used in a tank containing invertebrates such as prawns or sea anemones, because the copper quickly kills them.

Aquatic fungi sometimes attack the skin and fins producing an opaque film which may disappear if the water is changed. Persistent attacks can be treated by keeping the fishes for a few days in a solution of the fungicide griseofulvin (25 mg per litre).

Jerky swimming movements with the body in an oblique position, head up, indicate swimbladder trouble caused by inflammation, often resulting from a decrease in temperature. This often disappears if the water temperature is raised to 28–30°C. Some aquarists give the diseased fishes food soaked in aureomycin.

Distribution

The majority of marine aquarium fishes come from the coastal waters of the tropics, some from the Caribbean, but most from the coral reefs of the Indo-Pacific Ocean. This area extends from the Red Sea and East Africa through the warm parts of the Indian Ocean to Polynesia and Hawaii (Hawaiian marine fishes are somewhat different from others in the Indo-Pacific. In many cases separate species have evolved.) A few fishes from the Mediterranean are also suitable for the aquarium.

Marine fishes have similar requirements for diet and conditions so there is no individual list for each species. Symbols are given only for distribution as breeding is generally unsuccessful.

Family Canthigasteridae

Sharp-nosed puffers. About 12 species, all from the coral reefs of the Indo-Pacific and Atlantic. These slow-swimming fishes have only a limited ability to inflate the body to deter predators. The teeth are fused to form a parrot-like 'beak'.

Ocellated puffer

Canthigaster margaritatus

This puffer croaks and grunts when it is removed from the water. In the aquarium it is susceptible to frequent fungal attacks. No ventral fins. Indo-Pacific (except the Great Barrier Reef and Hawaii). *Length:* to 15 cm

Family Lutjanidae

The snappers: species in all warm seas. Most live in shoals near the sea-bed where they feed on crustaceans and small fishes. Some are caught for food, although a few species may have poisonous flesh.

Emperor snapper

Lutjanus sebae

The dorsal fin is pointed in the juveniles, rounded in the adults. Young individuals can be kept in the home aquarium where they eat almost anything and grow rapidly. Do not keep them with smaller fishes. Indo-Pacific (except Hawaii). *Length:* to 100 cm (only up to 30 cm in the aquarium)

Family Grammidae

Fairy basslets. A family of small colourful fishes living mainly in the crevices of coral reefs. Closely related to the Serranidae, from which they differ in having a broken lateral line.

Fairy basslet

Gramma loreto

Usually lives in underwater caves, always with the belly turned towards the nearest substrate—it may be seen upside-down beneath the roof of a cave. The female lays about 400 eggs in a nest of algae built by the male. The eggs are guarded by both parents until they hatch. Probably not yet bred in captivity. Western Caribbean, West Indies. *Length:* to 8 cm

Family Serranidae

The groupers: a family of about 400 species, found mostly in the tropics, a few in temperate areas. These hungry predators have large mouths and powerful teeth.

Six-lined grouper

Grammistes sexlineatus

Do not keep with smaller fishes. The number of pale longitudinal bands increases with age; juveniles have only three. In the aquarium this species can be fed on small crabs and earthworms. Lives among corals and in tidal pools. Red Sea, East Africa to Polynesia. *Length:* to 30 cm

Family Apogonidae

The cardinal fishes: small predators with species in all warm seas, particularly in the Indo-Pacific where there are more than 100 species. Some live among the spines of tropical sea-urchins where they feed on debris and thus act as cleaners (see Cleaner wrasse p 161). They have two separate dorsal fins.

Pyjama cardinal fish

Apogon nematopterus

Unlike most species in this family this is a peaceful fish. The eggs are incubated in the mouth of one of the parents, usually the male. Lives in small shoals in coral heads. East Africa to Melanesia. *Length:* to 8 cm

Family Holocentridae

The soldierfishes or squirrelfishes: small, attractively coloured nocturnal fishes with species in all warm seas. When young they can be kept in the home aquarium but not with smaller fishes. The eyes are large and the gill covers have sharp spines.

Crimson squirrelfish

Myripristis murdjan

Known in Queensland as the Blotch-eye. A relatively gregarious squirrelfish, living mostly in small shoals. It is eaten in Hawaii. Commonly found on coral reefs. East Africa, Red Sea, eastwards to Tahiti. *Length:* to 30 cm

Family Sciaenidae

Drums and croakers. Medium-sized, predatory, shoaling fishes living on coral reefs or in coastal waters of warm seas. The popular name refers to their ability to produce sounds by the rapid vibration of special muscles.

Cubbyu

Equetus acuminatus

Also known as the High hat. It has been known to spawn in the aquarium after very active chasing (the pair swims around in circles), although the eggs have never been hatched successfully. South Carolina, Bermuda to Rio de Janeiro. *Length:* to 30 cm (only up to 15 cm in the aquarium)

Jack-knife fish

Equetus lanceolatus

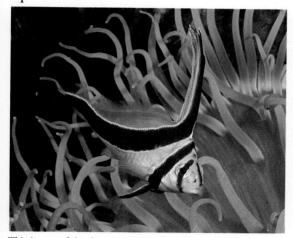

This is one of the drums that lives in deeper water. It is a good fish for the aquarium although it does tend to hide away behind the rocks. Feeds mainly on crustaceans. South Carolina, Bermuda to Brazil. *Length:* to 25 cm

Family Muraenidae

A large family of naked (scaleless), tough-skinned, predatory eels with species in tropical and sub-tropical areas. They live mostly in crevices in rocks or corals, from which they come out to take prey. They have sharp teeth and are likely to bite the hand of the unwary diver or aquarist.

Starry moray eel

Echidna nebulosa

A mainly nocturnal fish, living by day in rock crevices. It can give a painful bite which may result in infection, although no venom is involved. Found in shallow lagoons in coral-reef areas. Red Sea to Hawaii. *Length:* to 75 cm

Family Pomadasyidae

The sweetlips, or thick-lipped grunters, occur only on the coral reefs of the Indo-Pacific. They are omnivorous and the adults have thick fleshy lips. They undergo marked changes in coloration with age.

Harlequin sweetlips

Plectorhynchus chaetodontoides

In the young the body is brown with areas of white edged wih dark brown. The adults are speckled. Suitable for the aquarium only when young. East Africa to East Indies, The Philippines, Melanesia and Tahiti. *Length:* to 45 cm

Oriental sweetlips

Plectorhynchus orientalis

In the young the body is chocolate-brown with areas of pale cream edged with yellow. The adults have cream and brown longitudinal stripes but vary considerably from one individual to another. Suitable for the aquarium only when young. East Africa, Seychelles to East Indies and Melanesia. *Length:* to 40 cm

Family Mullidae

The red mullets or surmullets: a large family of bottom-living fishes from tropical and subtropical seas. Most of them are red or yellowish. There is a pair of fleshy barbels under the chin.

Red mullet

Mullus surmuletus

This fish is more often eaten than kept in the aquarium (where it is not easy to keep). It can be fed on small earthworms and chopped prawns. Mainly subtropical, occurring as far north as the southern part of the North Sea: it even breeds in the English Channel. Eastern Atlantic, Mediterranean, Black Sea. *Length:* to 40 cm

Family Zanclidae

This family has only one species which lives in small shoals among corals. It is revered by Moslem fishermen in some areas.

Moorish idol

Zanclus canescens

Sometimes confused with the Pennant coralfish. The 'horn' above the eye becomes larger with age. Indo-Pacific (as far east as the Pacific coast of Mexico). *Length:* to 22 cm

Family Chaetodontidae

The butterflyfishes and angelfishes: a family of small to medium-sized fishes which live in shallow water among corals. Most come from the Indo-Pacific, but some are from the Caribbean and tropical Atlantic. The juveniles of some marine angelfishes have a completely different pattern from that of the adults.

Pennant coralfish

Heniochus acuminatus

Also known as the Coachman, this is one of the most widely distributed of the coralfishes. Lives in pairs or in a small shoal. Red Sea to Queensland and Hawaii. *Length:* to 25 cm

Long-snouted coralfish

Forcipiger longirostris

Known in Queensland as the Longbill. A widely distributed species usually living in pairs or small groups. The long snout enables it to search for small worms and crustaceans living in the crevices of a coral reef. It is not easy to keep in the aquarium and it may take a long time to become accustomed to taking food that floats in the water. Red Sea to Australia and Hawaii. *Length:* to 18 cm

Long-nosed butterflyfish

Chelmon rostratus

Lives in pairs or small groups. Not an easy fish to keep in the aquarium. It will eat small marine crustaceans and sometimes small earthworms. It is often aggressive towards other members of its own species. Red Sea to south-east Asia, China, The Philippines, Australia and Melanesia. *Length:* to 17 cm

Threadfin coralfish

Chaetodon auriga

One of the hardier members of the genus *Chaetodon* and one of the most suitable for the aquarium, although it is often aggressive towards other members of its own species. The dorsal fin of the adults carries a long filament above the eyespot. Red Sea to Queensland and Hawaii. *Length:* to 23 cm

Pearl-scale butterflyfish

Chaetodon chrysurus

A very variable butterflyfish with several local races. Recorded mainly from the coasts of East Africa, the Seychelles and Madagascar. *Length:* to 15 cm

Vagabond coralfish

Chaetodon vagabundus

Also known as the Criss-cross butterflyfish. This species is not confined to coral reefs; it is often found in lagoons. It is one of the most abundant butterflyfishes and was first named and described by Linnaeus in 1758. In young individuals there is a large black eyespot on the dorsal fin and a dark stripe running across the dorsal and anal fins. Tropical Indo-Pacific (except Hawaii). *Length:* to 20 cm

Collared coralfish

Chaetodon collaris

One of the most frequently imported species. It is usually not difficult to keep in the aquarium, where it will eat small crustaceans, mosquito larvae, and *Tubifex*. It has even been known to eat dried food. India, Sri Lanka, East Indies, The Philippines and southern China. *Length:* to 15 cm

145

Klein's coralfish

Chaetodon kleini

This species is not very often imported for the aquarium, but it has been kept successfully. East Africa and Seychelles to The Philippines, Melanesia, Queensland, Fiji and Samoa. *Length:* to 13 cm

Saddled coralfish

Chaetodon ephippium

This is not an easy species to keep in the aquarium: it is susceptible to disease and difficult to get to feed. Very young specimens lack the dorsal filament but have a broad stripe through each eye, which becomes less conspicuous with age. The Philippines, East Indies, Melanesia, Queensland, Polynesia, Hawaii. *Length:* to 30 cm

Red-striped coralfish

Chaetodon lunula

The juveniles are often found in tidal pools on rocky shores and these are particularly suitable for the home aquarium. They have a black spot on the dorsal fin; the adults have oblique markings on the flanks. South-east Asia, south Pacific, Hawaii. *Length:* to 20 cm

Spotfin butterflyfish

Chaetodon ocellatus

In the aquarium this fish is usually hardier than many other butterflyfishes. It should be kept in a small shoal and fed on live food such as shrimps and mussels but it has been kept successfully on a diet of dried food. Massachusetts to West Indies and Brazil. *Length:* to 14 cm

Black-backed coralfish

Chaetodon melanotus

In old individuals the colours become duller, the ring at the base of the tail is broken up and the black spot at the base of the anal fin becomes much reduced. Not often imported and a difficult species to keep in the aquarium. A common species off East Africa, Seychelles eastwards to The Philippines, Melanesia, Queensland, Fiji, Samoa. *Length:* to 17 cm

Imperial angelfish

Pomacanthodes imperator

A rather uncommon marine angelfish. The juveniles are black with a pattern of white stripes on the head and flanks, with some blue stripes. The stripes become curved towards the rear. Red Sea to Hawaii and Queensland. *Length:* to 36 cm

Blue angelfish

Pomacanthops semicirculatus

A very variable species. In some juveniles the blue markings on the caudal fin have been likened to Arabic script and have even been interpreted as verses from the Koran, so the species is highly venerated by Moslem fishermen in certain areas. Indo-Pacific (except Hawaii). *Length:* to 36 cm

Grey angelfish

Pomacanthus arcuatus

Usually difficult to keep in the aquarium. The tank should have a good growth of algae which form an important part of the diet in the wild. They will also eat brine shrimps, *Tubifex* and chopped earthworms. The juveniles are similar in appearance to those of the French angelfish. New Jersey to West Indies, southwards to Rio de Janeiro. *Length:* to 40 cm

French angelfish

Pomacanthus paru

The juveniles are black with four vertical yellow stripes and a ring of yellow on the tail. This species can be kept in the same way as the Grey angelfish. Coasts of the tropical Atlantic. *Length:* to 40 cm

Rock beauty

Holacanthus tricolor

This is a rather delicate fish in the aquarium. It should be fed like the Grey angelfish. When about 2 cm long it is completely yellow except for a dark spot on the rear part of the back. As it grows this marking increases in size until it covers the dorsal and anal fins and most of the body. Georgia, Bermuda to West Indies. *Length:* to 60 cm

150

Royal empress angelfish

Pygoplites diacanthus

A beautiful but rarely imported angelfish, which lives in shallow waters in the wild. Keep in a tank with plenty of hiding places for this is a shy species, particularly when young. Indo-Pacific (except Hawaii). *Length:* to 22 cm

Blue-girdled angelfish

Euxiphipops navarchus

In its natural range this colourful fish lives in the calm water areas of coral reefs, either solitarily or in pairs. Keep in a spacious tank, either alone or with other peaceful fishes. It can be fed on *Tubifex*, brine shrimps, chopped fish and prawns, but it must have a supplement of plant food (such as finely chopped lettuce). The Philippines, Indonesia, Melanesia. *Length:* to 20 cm

Dusky angelfish

Centropyge bispinosus

These fishes usually settle down well in the aquarium and are not difficult to feed. In the wild they often browse on algae. Unlike the larger marine angelfishes the juvenile patterns of *Centropyge* species are similar to those of the adults. East Africa, Seychelles, various localities in the western Pacific. *Length:* to 11 cm

Lemon-peel

Centropyge flavissimus

The juveniles are marked with a black spot on the middle of each flank below the lateral line. The related *C. heraldi* from Japan does not have the blue markings. Recorded mainly from the South Pacific (New Hebrides, Queensland, Fiji, Tahiti). *Length:* to 10 cm

Black angelfish

Centropyge tibicen

The adults are usually black with a brownish head and a large yellow marking on the centre of each flank. The juveniles are similarly coloured but the flank markings are white. South-east Asia, Taiwan, The Philippines, New Guinea, New Hebrides. *Length:* to 13 cm

Family Pomacentridae

Damselfishes. This is a large family of small fishes which live in small groups on coral reefs and in rocky shore areas in all warm seas. Many species are very colourful and are popular in the aquarium.

Blue puller

Chromis caeruleus

These damselfishes are commonly found living in close-knit shoals of 20–25 individuals around coral heads on the reefs, from which they do not stray far. Juveniles in particular live in among the coral tentacles. Indo-Pacific (except Hawaii). *Length:* to 12 cm

Demoiselle

Chromis chromis

This species is commonly seen on rocky shores and in harbours. It is a good fish for a subtropical tank (kept at about 18°C). The male establishes a territory, which he defends vigorously. He swims up to a female and spreads out his fins in display. The female lays eggs on a stone previously cleaned by the male, who then sheds sperm over them. The eggs are tended by the male. Portugal to West Africa, Mediterranean, Black Sea. *Length:* to 12 cm

White-tailed humbug

Dascyllus aruanus

Another common damselfish which exhibits marked territorial behaviour, so it may be difficult to keep more than a few in an aquarium of about 100 cm in length. They have often been observed diving among the tentacles of sea anemones. This and other species of *Dascyllus* have spawned in the aquarium but the fry have seldom been reared. Indo-Pacific (except Hawaii). *Length:* to 8 cm

Black-tailed humbug

IP

Dascyllus melanurus

This is one of the better species for a tropical marine tank. It can be fed on a varied diet, mainly of live food but can also be accustomed to taking dried foods. South-east Asia, The Philippines, Queensland (very abundant on Great Barrier Reef), east to Melanesia. *Length:* to 7 cm

Grey humbug

IP

Dascyllus reticulatus

The male has been seen to clean algae or debris from a piece of dead coral and then to court a near-by female. She lays her eggs on the prepared spawning site and is then chased away by the male. He guards the eggs until they hatch in about 4 days. Indo-Pacific (except Hawaii and Red Sea). *Length:* to 12 cm

White-spot humbug

Dascyllus trimaculatus

The white spots are particularly conspicuous in the juveniles but they usually disappear with age. Old individuals have brownish coloration on the underside. The juveniles are often seen in among the tentacles of tropical soft corals (i.e. those which do not build a calcareous skeleton). The adults swim near the corals. In the aquarium they will feed on freeze-dried foods. Indo-Pacific (except Hawaii). *Length:* to 12 cm

Blue-banded sergeant-major

Abudefduf oxyodon

When young this very handsome damselfish lives in small shoals, which tend to break up as the fishes age. The adults live either in pairs or on their own. In the aquarium this fish has the reputation of being particularly aggressive towards others of its own species. South-east Asia, Taiwan, The Philippines. *Length:* to 8 cm

Five-banded sergeant-major

Abudefduf saxatilis

One of the most widely distributed of all tropical marine fishes. The adults are seen swimming in shoals in shallow water, where they feed on invertebrates and algae. The juveniles live mainly in small shoals in tidal pools. Indo-Pacific (except Hawaii), Atlantic, Caribbean (common on reefs). *Length:* to 18 cm

Family Amphiprionidae

Anemone-fishes or clownfishes. A family of small, colourful fishes found only in the Indo-Pacific, excluding Hawaii. In the wild, clownfishes always live in association with certain large sea anemones, but are not killed by the sting-cells on the tentacles because they have a special mucus covering their bodies. Other fishes of the same size would be caught. In the aquarium clownfishes can be kept without a sea anemone.

Tomato clownfish

Premnas biaculeatus

The sharp spine just behind each eye is characteristic of this species. South-east Asia, The Philippines, Queensland, eastwards to Melanesia. *Length:* to 15 cm

Black-finned clownfish

IP

Amphiprion percula

This is probably the most commonly imported member of the genus *Amphiprion* but it is rather susceptible to infection. It has been bred on a few occasions in the aquarium. The female lays 150–200 eggs and these are guarded by the male until they hatch in about 10 days. There is still some confusion between this species and the very similar *A. ocellaris*. Queensland, Melanesia. *Length:* to 8 cm

Yellow-tailed clownfish

IP

Amphiprion sebae

This is a hardy species which will thrive in the aquarium better than *A. percula*. If juveniles are kept they should be fed several times a day and they will then grow rapidly. Arabia, India, Sri Lanka, Indonesia. *Length:* to 12 cm

Allen's clownfish

Amphiprion sandaracinos

This is one of the few clownfishes that has spawned in the aquarium. They form closely knit pairs; both partners guard the eggs. This species was first described as recently as 1972. The Philippines. *Length:* to 8 cm

Salmon clownfish

Amphiprion perideraion

Similar in shape to *A. sandaracinos*, but with a thin pale band running across the gill cover. This species is usually rather delicate in the aquarium. South-east Asia, Hong Kong, Taiwan, The Philippines, New Guinea, Queensland, New Hebrides. *Length:* to 8 cm

Family Labridae

Wrasses. A large family of small and medium-sized fishes found in all temperate and tropical seas. Some show changes in coloration with age. The lips are thick and fleshy and the sharp teeth are used by many species for crushing molluscs.

Tomato wrasse

Coris gaimardi

Only small specimens are suitable for the home aquarium. Up to a length of about 6 cm they are red with areas of white edged with black. Some species of *Coris* spend the night on the bottom, often resting on their sides. Indo-Pacific (except Queensland). *Length:* to 30 cm

Coris aygula

Also known as *Coris angulata*. This species is suitable for the aquarium only when young. At a length of about 12 cm the large red blotches disappear. Old individuals are dark green. They like to bury themselves at night—a habit shared with other wrasses—so the tank should have a sand substrate. Indo-Pacific (except Queensland and Hawaii). *Length:* to 100 cm

Cleaner wrasse

Labroides dimidiatus

This wrasse removes scraps of dead skin and parasites from the mouth, teeth, body and gills of other fishes which have been seen to queue up for its services. It approaches its clients with a wriggling movement and has even been seen inside the mouth of large predatory fishes. Beware of buying the very similar Sabre-toothed blenny (p 170) which bites chunks out of other fishes. Indo-Pacific (except Hawaii). *Length:* to 10 cm

Six-lined wrasse

Pseudocheilinus hexataenia

When small, a number of these wrasses can be kept together but not with other larger species. They should be fed on brine shrimps and freeze-dried food. On the reefs this wrasse lives solitarily and feeds on the sea-bed near coral heads, taking small crustaceans and worms. East Africa, Red Sea to south-east Asia, The Philippines, Tuamotu Islands. *Length:* to 45 cm

Bluehead

Thalassoma bifasciatum

Smaller specimens are yellow with a black stripe; these may be males or females. The males change colour and acquire the blue head. The young act as cleaners, taking parasites off the skin of other fishes. Bermuda, Florida, West Indies. *Length:* to 15 cm

Moon wrasse

Thalassoma lunare

Do not keep this predatory species with smaller fishes. At spawning time the male chases the female very actively. She lays several hundred eggs, which rise to the surface. There is no record of the young being reared in the aquarium. Indian Ocean eastwards to Hong Kong, The Philippines, New Guinea, Solomon Islands, Queensland and New Hebrides. *Length:* to 30 cm

Family Acanthuridae

Surgeonfishes. This family occurs in all warm seas; there are about 60 species in the Indo-Pacific. The name refers to two sharp, bony 'scalpels', one on each side of the caudal peduncle, which can be erected to form weapons. They are vegetarian and feed mainly on algae.

Flag-tailed surgeonfish

Paracanthurus hepatus

One of the most handsome surgeonfishes. Becomes less colourful with age but still has blue on the head. Indo-Pacific (except Hawaii). *Length:* to 25 cm

White-cheeked surgeonfish

Acanthurus glaucopareius

On the reefs this surgeonfish feeds almost entirely on the delicate algae that grow on dead coral heads. Allow algae to grow in the tank. South-east Asia, Pacific to west coast of central America. *Length:* to 26 cm

White-breasted surgeonfish

Acanthurus leucosternon

The diet should include large amounts of plant matter to supplement the algae growing in the tank. Care must be taken as this may lead to fouling of the water. East Africa, Seychelles, India, Sri Lanka. *Length:* to 22 cm

Yellow-tailed sailfin-tang

Zebrasoma xanthurum

This species has very rough scales on the head and body. Specimens from the Red Sea are bluer than those from further east. East Africa, Red Sea, Persian Gulf, India and Sri Lanka. *Length:* to 20 cm

Sailfin-tang

Zebrasoma veliferum

This is usually regarded as the most suitable surgeonfish for the aquarium. Although not so colourful as its relatives, it is extremely handsome when the dorsal and anal fins are raised. Only young specimens should be bought: they usually settle down well. Indo-Pacific. *Length:* to 40 cm

Family Balistidae

Triggerfishes: a family of about 30 species, distributed in all warm seas. Most have poisonous flesh.

Trigger mechanism
The dorsal fin consists of three spines. When raised the first spine can be locked into position by the second spine. This allows the fish to wedge itself into narrow rock crevices. When not in use, the spine folds back into a groove

White-blotched triggerfish

Balistoides niger

Small specimens are suitable for the home aquarium. They will feed on brine shrimps and on freeze-dried foods. East Africa, Madagascar to Melanesia and Queensland. *Length:* to 50 cm

Odonus niger

Also known as the Black triggerfish. This species has red teeth. The fins are tall and the caudal fin lobes are elongated. Mating attempts have been observed in the aquarium although they have been unsuccessful so far as is known. Atlantic, Indo-Pacific. *Length:* to 50 cm

Picasso fish

Rhinecanthus aculeatus

Known in Hawaii as *humu-humu-nuku-nuku-a-pua'a*. This is a good aquarium fish when small; it becomes very aggressive with age and may attack other fishes. It will eat worms, (including *Tubifex*), crabs, brine shrimps and other invertebrates. Indo-Pacific. *Length:* to 30 cm

Family Aluteridae

The filefishes or leatherjackets are small to medium-sized fishes with species in all temperate and tropical seas—the majority in the Indo-Pacific. They have a similar trigger mechanism to that of the family Balistidae (p 165). There are no ventral fins and the scales are small and rough.

Beaked leatherjacket

Oxymonacanthus longirostris

In the wild this fish feeds head down on coral polyps and it does not adapt easily to feeding in the aquarium. Keep in a small group. East Africa, Seychelles, south-east Asia, The Philippines, Queensland, South Pacific. *Length:* to 8 cm

Family Ostraciidae (= Ostraciontidae)

The boxfishes or cowfishes are found in all warm seas. They are small, scaleless fishes. The head and body are encased in an armour of hard, bony plates. They move slowly, propelled by undulations of the dorsal and anal fins and steered by the tail. They may release substances that are poisonous to other fishes, so they must be kept in a tank on their own.

Blue boxfish

Ostracion meleagris

Also known as the Spotted boxfish. This species shows sexual dimorphism: the male is bluish with orange blotches, the female is black with smaller white spots. This is not always an easy fish to keep. East Africa to south-east Asia, The Philippines, Hawaii, Melanesia and Tahiti. *Length:* to 22 cm

Long-horned cowfish

Lactoria cornuta

This odd-looking fish lives in shallow waters among marine vegetation in the wild. It has been bred in the aquarium. The eggs rise to the surface and hatch in about 5 days. The fry can be reared on microscopic marine organisms and later on brine shrimps. The adults browse on algae. Indo-Pacific (except Hawaii). *Length:* to 50 cm

Family Opistognathidae

Jawfishes. A small family of bottom-living fishes, often found among coral debris. The mouth is large and protrusible and the jaws are used to dig a burrow which it sometimes inhabits with a prawn. The two have a special association, often sharing the same food.

Yellowhead jawfish

Opistognathus aurifrons

This fish spends the day near the mouth of its burrow, snapping up any small animals that pass by. Spawning has taken place in the aquarium but it is unlikely that the young have been reared successfully. It is a mouthbrooder. Florida, West Indies. *Length:* to 10 cm

Family Diodontidae

Porcupinefishes. About 18 species, found in all warm seas. When alarmed they inflate themselves with air or water and the spines are then erected, making the fish an unattractive mouthful.

Spotted porcupinefish

Diodon hystrix

This odd-looking fish has protruding eyes which can be turned in all directions, giving a very wide field of vision. The jaws are particularly powerful and in the wild it uses them to feed on crabs, sea-snails, sea-urchins and other hard-shelled animals. When inflated it is often washed up on tropical shores, where it can be collected as an ornament. Atlantic, Indo-Pacific. *Length:* to 90 cm

Family Blenniidae

Blennies. A large family of carnivorous fishes found in all tropical and temperate seas. Some come out on land for short periods. The eggs are laid in a small cave or an empty mollusc shell and guarded until they hatch. Blennies are easy to keep in the aquarium but most are not very colourful.

Sabre-toothed blenny

Aspidontus taeniatus

Also known as the False cleaner, this fish is a remarkable mimic of the Cleaner wrasse (p 161). It uses this attribute to approach other fishes which it then attacks. Keep in a tank on its own. South-east Asia, The Philippines to Solomon Islands, Samoa and Tahiti. *Length:* to 13 cm

Family Gobiidae

A very large family of small fishes. In tropical seas they are particularly abundant on coral reefs. In temperate areas they are commonly seen in tidal pools. A few live in fresh waters. The ventral fins are united to form a suction disc.

Yellow coral-goby

Gobiodon citrinus

This colourful goby lives in coral heads. It feeds on worms and other invertebrates and on fish eggs spawned above the corals. It should be kept in a tank on its own. East Africa, Red Sea to Solomon Islands and Fiji. *Length:* to 5.5 cm

Neon goby

Gobiosoma oceanops

Pattern and coloration are similar to the Cleaner wrasse (p 161) and this fish also acts as a cleaner. It has been bred in the aquarium. The eggs are laid in small burrows and guarded by both parents. Southern Florida, West Indies. *Length:* to 6 cm

Family Scorpaenidae

Scorpionfishes and dragonfishes. This large family is found in all temperate and tropical seas, some on rocky coasts and coral reefs, others in deep water. On the reefs they lie in wait for their prey, mostly other fishes. They carry poisonous spines, which can be extremely dangerous.

Dendrochirus brachypterus

This scorpionfish is commonly found in shallow water among coral rubble. It will readily take small live fishes but will also eat dead food. Indo-Pacific (except Great Barrier Reef). *Length:* to 17 cm

Dragonfish

Pterois volitans

Also known as the Lionfish or Turkeyfish. This is now a common aquarium fish which should only be kept with larger fishes. It has a good appetite and can be accustomed to taking dead food. The spines of the dorsal, anal and ventral fins are equipped with venom glands. Indo-Pacific (except Hawaii). *Length:* to 35 cm

Family Plotosidae

Elongated catfishes. Most live in the sea, unlike the numerous freshwater (mainly tropical) catfish families. They have a scaleless, slimy skin and 4 pairs of barbels. The serrated spine at the front of the dorsal and pectoral fins can inflict painful wounds.

Striped catfish

Plotosus anguillaris

These catfishes move across the sea-bed in closely packed shoals. In the aquarium they should be kept in a group. Old specimens become aggressive towards other fishes. East Africa, Red Sea to Japan, Queensland, Melanesia and Polynesia. *Length:* to 70 cm

Family Platacidae

Batfishes. A family of tall-bodied fishes which live in coastal waters; the juveniles are sometimes seen in estuaries. When young the dorsal and anal fins are very long, but they become relatively shorter with age. Seen from the side the body is almost circular.

Batfish

Platax pinnatus

The fishes known as *P. orbicularis* and *P. teira* are here regarded as forms of this variable species. It is an attractive fish for the home aquarium when young but grows rapidly when well fed and will soon outgrow its tank. Keep fishes of a similar size in a small group. Indo-Pacific (except Hawaii). *Length:* to 60 cm

Family Callionymidae

Dragonets. Small fishes which live on or near the sea-bed in shallow coastal waters, mainly in the tropics, a few in temperate areas. The body is elongated, and there are no scales.

Mandarin fish

Synchiropus splendidus

The front rays of the dorsal fin are elongated in the male. This is a difficult fish for the aquarium. Keep it in a species tank and feed it on small worms and crustaceans. South-east Asia, The Philippines, Queensland and Melanesia. *Length:* to 10 cm

Family Centriscidae

Razorfishes or shrimpfishes. These thin, almost transparent tropical fishes live in small shoals and swim in a vertical position, head down. The spine at the rear belongs to the first dorsal fin; the soft dorsal and the caudal fin are positioned ventrally.

Razorfish

Aeoliscus strigatus

Also known as the Shrimpfish. This odd fish is often seen, head down, among the long spines of certain sea-urchins. The underside of the body is thin and razor-like. Seychelles to southeast Asia, Hawaii and Melanesia. *Length:* to 12 cm

Family Syngnathidae

Pipefishes and sea-horses. Several species of sea-horse are found mostly in warm seas; pipefishes are also found in temperate areas. They have bony armour and small fins. The caudal fin is absent in some species, while in the sea-horses the tail is prehensile, allowing the fish to attach itself to seaweed. The eggs are laid in a pouch or in a special area on the ventral surface of the male. The young are extremely difficult to feed, requiring tiny amounts of newly hatched brine shrimp nauplii.

Golden sea-horse

Hippocampus kuda

Coloration varies from brownish to lemon-yellow. The male has a brood pouch under the tail. Sea-horses are not easy to keep as they will not eat dead or dried food. Their tubular snouts end in a small mouth, so they must be given suitably small food, such as brine shrimps, mosquito larvae or newly hatched fish fry. Indo-Pacific. *Length:* to 30 cm

Glossary

Adipose fin Small rayless fleshy fin between dorsal and caudal fins

Algae Primitive aquatic plants, mostly microscopic

Anal fin Unpaired fin between anus and tail. See p 5

Barbels Sensory appendages on the upper and/or lower jaw

Brine shrimp (*Artemia salina*) Small crustaceans used as food. The early larval stage (nauplius) is a valuable food for fish fry. See p 10

Caudal fin Tail fin. See p 5

Caudal peduncle Root of the tail. See p 5

°DH Denotes degree of water hardness (German scale). See p 6

Dorsal Of the back, hence dorsal fin or fins. See p 5

Electric organ Modified muscles producing electric pulses

Free-swimming Used of fish fry that start swimming after consuming the contents of the yolk sac

Gills Respiratory structure. See p 5

Gonopodium Copulatory organ formed from the anal fin

Infusorians Collective term for microscopic organisms

Invertebrates Animals without backbones

Lateral line Sensory organ along the flanks of fishes. See p 5

Live-bearing Of fishes which produce live young

Nauplius (pl, nauplii) Early larval stage of some crustaceans

Operculum Gill cover

Ovipositor Egg-laying organ (e.g., in female Bitterling)

Pectoral Of the breast

Pectoral fins Paired fins lying behind the gills. See p 5

pH (*pondus Hydrogenii*—weight of hydrogen) Denotes the acidity or alkalinity of the water. See p 6

Planarians Small free-living (i.e., non-parasitic) flatworms

Plankton Collective term for animals and plants drifting passively in the sea and fresh water. Most are microscopic

Polyp The living part of a coral

Protozoan One-celled, microscopic animals (e.g., *Paramecium*)

Rotifers Wheel animalcules. A group of minute aquatic animals, valuable as food for fish fry. See p 10

Spermatophore Small packet of sperm

Substrate In the aquarium, the gravel or sand on the tank bottom

Swimbladder Gas-filled sac positioned dorsally in the body cavity

Transverse Of cross bars on the flank of a fish

Tubercle (nuptial tubercle) Small wart-like protuberance appearing on certain fishes at spawning time

Tubifex Small red worms living in river mud, used as live food

Ventral Of the underside or belly, hence ventral fins

Conversion tables

Conversions are approximate

Length

ft/in	3/8 in	3/4 in	1 1/8 in	1 1/2 in	2 in	2 3/8 in	2 3/4 in	3 1/8 in	3 1/2 in	4 in	8 in	1 ft	3 ft 4 in
cm	1	2	3	4	5	6	7	8	9	10	20	50	100

Temperature

°C	5	10	15	20	21	22	23	24	25	26	27	28	29	30
°F	41	50	59	68	70	72	73	75	77	79	81	82	84	86

Volume

Metric	1 litre	10 litres	50 litres	100 litres
Imperial	1¾ pints	2 gal	11 gal	22 gal
US	2 pints	2½ gal	12½ gal	25 gal

Index

177